HMS LI WO:

THE MOST DECORATED SMALL SHIP

IN THE NAVY

HMS LI WO:

THE MOST DECORATED SMALL SHIP

IN THE NAVY

A.V. SELLWOOD

AMBERLEY

Amberley Publishing
The Hill, Stroud
Gloucestershire, GL5 4EP

www.amberley-books.com

British Library Cataloguing in Publication Data.
A catalogue record for this book is available from the British Library.

ISBN 978 1 4456 4794 4 (print)
ISBN 978 1 4456 4795 1 (ebook)

Typeset in 10pt on 12pt Sabon.
Typesetting and Origination by Amberley Publishing.
Printed in the UK.

Contents

Stand by to Die

Although I was only about nine or ten years old at the time, I still clearly remember my late father repeating the words, 'The most decorated small ship in the navy', again and again as he wrote the story of HMS *Li Wo*, and of her truly heroic but doomed battle against odds. I was impressed, as any boy would be, by such heroism; but his continued repetition of 'The most decorated small ship in the navy' told me that he was too. Having first been alerted to the story by an unusual posthumous Victoria Cross citation in the Admiralty archives, he set out to track down the few surviving members of her crew, and this book was the result.

After beating off Japanese air attacks while attempting to reach Dutch-held Java, HMS *Li Wo* went into battle alone against an entire Japanese invasion fleet; but she was not a battleship or cruiser or destroyer, not even an MTB. She was a formerly peaceful Yangtse river steamer converted into a so-called 'patrol vessel' by the simple addition of an ancient (ironically Japanese made) single four-inch gun and two Lewis machine-guns. Neither was she cornered or trapped by the Sumatra-bound invaders, which seemed to be ignoring her. Escape was probably possible by hiding among the islands. But she did not choose escape.

Led by an RNR Captain (Lt Wilkinson VC, RNR), an Australian First Officer and a New Zealander Gunnery Officer, her crew consisted mainly of some Chinese stokers, some survivors from the recently sunk battlecruisers HMS *Repulse* and *Prince of Wales* and a smattering of soldiers and airmen she had taken on at Singapore just before it fell. Instead of attempting escape, her captain held a quick straw poll of his crew, hoisted two battle ensigns and went to the attack. By the time the battle ended, HMS *Li Wo* was a burning, sinking hulk hit by numerous shells from an escorting cruiser and destroyer; but so too was a fully laden Japanese troopship she had shelled and set alight and rammed; a troopship that was abandoned by the troops she carried and her crew, burned through most of the night, and had sunk by dawn.

I must have read and re-read this story at least half a dozen times since it was first published back in 1961, and each time I am struck not only by the story itself of the little ship and its very few survivors, but also by my late father's way of telling it. *Stand by to Die* was the last of four he wrote about the war at sea, the earlier ones being *Atlantis*, *Dynamite for Hire* and *HMS Electra*, following which he went on to write a number of other books about modern history while working full-time as a journalist. My only regret regarding his writing and journalism is that, as a result, he had fewer hours to spend with my three sisters and me than we would have liked; but what time he was able to spend with us and my Mum was always full of love and adventure.

Robert Sellwood
2015

CHAPTER ONE

HMS *Showboat*

'The sooner they tell us to scarper,' the AB said, 'the better yours truly will like it.'

'Which goes for me, too,' thought Stanton, but he kept his thoughts to himself.

From the first lieutenant of this dumpy little river steamer they had turned into a 'warship' – this former Yangtse trader with the odd-sounding Chinese name and the crew of many races – such sentiments, he reflected, might sound a little defeatist. Guts were needed.

All through the late afternoon, while the island burned around them, the men of the *Li Wo* had been storing and bunkering their ship. Some said, the hopeful ones, to make a getaway; but others, the vast majority, took a rather cynical view.

That shower of brass-bound and bomb-proof bastards at HQ had detained the ship so long in local waters that they would never let her go.

The feeling that inspired this multi-lingual bind, in English, Malay and Chinese, would have shocked armchair patriots back home, talking of making Singapore a Stalingrad.

On the spot it seemed rather different.

The bulk of the regular warships had long since left, to regroup in far-away Batavia and Ceylon. The remnants of the Air Force had withdrawn to Sumatra. The army, cut to shreds during its fighting retreat from the frontiers of Siam, was in places little more than a disorganised armed mob. Only Whitehall's disapproval, it was said, prevented the bomb-racked, fever-threatened city, crowded with refugees, from capitulating by dawn.

So what the hell difference could the *Li Wo*'s presence make? Ask me another, thought Stanton wearily.

Sixty-five days now since the onslaught on Pearl Harbour ... sixty-four since the sinking of Britain's *Prince of Wales* and *Repulse*, bombed in the steaming Gulf of Siam. Sixty-four days ... and yet it seemed a lifetime.

On shore, the Japanese had advanced four hundred miles. Never slackening the violent pace they'd first set in the bloody waters of Slim River, their burp-gunners were now amok in the suburbs of Singapore itself.

At sea, the Imperial Navy, all the odds in its favour, had switched from supporting the army to a more predatory role: and one didn't have to look far for the result.

The waters of the anchorage, which through the dark hours had reflected flares and flame, had changed to muddy brown, the surface shrouded by a blanket of spilled fuel oil and the wreckage of refugee sampans which had sailed to 'safety' only the night before.

The trap was springing shut, and the weary men knew it.

The enemy, triumphant on land, were gathering force behind them, on the sea.

'The flag that braved a thousand years the battle and the breeze ...'

The words of the poem, learned twenty years before unwillingly at school, returned suddenly to Ronald Stanton, and with such preposterous incongruity that they almost made him laugh.

A dirty, tattered White Ensign drooped from the *Li Wo*'s round stem, as alien to the ship as the HMS before her name or the title of RNR (Temp.) given to her officers.

The flag hung listlessly and dejectedly, stirring only when forced into a flurry of movement by a puff of hot wind from the shore. It clung to its staff with a sort of desperate bewilderment, like a drunk reaching wildly for a lamp-post. No sign of heroics here!

'HMS *Showboat*' was what naval wits had christened the *Li Wo*, requisitioned from the Indo China Steam Navigation Company in the days before Pearl Harbour. And even now the nickname seemed to fit.

Though sturdily built, extremely manoeuvrable, and launched as recently as 1935, the little ship would not have looked unduly out of place on the Mississippi of the 1860s.

Her beam was matronly, her superstructure top-heavy ... a triple tier of box-like cabins extended like a sugarcake for two-thirds of her length. Not even the four-inch gun – antique and stamped 'Made in Japan' – installed offensively on a platform below the bridge could disguise her peaceable origin.

'Yet, here you are, you poor lost thing,' mused Stanton, 'bang in the centre of a military volcano.'

'The flag that braved a thousand years ...' How did the rest of it run?

But he'd only got to the somewhat discouraging point of recalling that though the deck was the English mariners' field of fame, 'the ocean was their grave' when he was rudely interrupted.

'High time we got moving.'

A rating stood beside him, squinting dully and creasing his eyes suspiciously as though peering into the sun.

'I said,' repeated the rating, 'that it's high time we got moving.'

His omission of the 'sir' was deliberate, as if to emphasise the bitterness of his complaint. The woman tattooed on his bare chest writhed as he breathed, before the officer's fascinated eyes. Another man chimed in: 'Must 'ave gone mad on the island, holding us here like this. When the hell do we get clearance?'

Stanton wiped the sweat from under his armpits with the back of his hand and snapped: 'Pipe down, you. We'll get out when they tell us to, no sooner, no later. Meanwhile you go back to duty.'

The two ratings slunk off.

Morale was low, and tempers frayed to the limit.

Tom Wilkinson, the *Li Wo*'s master, appeared on the bridge, sniffed at the air, scowled round and cursed the planners at Fort Canning, now the Island's GHQ, from the bottom of his heavily laden heart.

A tough Lancashire man, 'Wilkie', as he was known in every port in China, had been heard to say that the Nips and their frightfulness never bothered him a bit. For all their effect on him they might as well stay at home and save themselves the trouble.

Nor was he boasting: he was merely stating a fact. Few things really troubled Wilkinson, except the pig-headedness of those who were fools enough to oppose his stubborn prejudices.

Not many did.

For Wilkinson, like his ship, bore the stamp of an earlier era. He was as tough as the toughest shellback of the grand old days of sail.

Incredible efficiency, hard grind and ruthless energy; from starting as a boy in a trading schooner he'd come up the hard way, and stayed hard ever since.

'And yet,' whispered the quartermaster, on the look-out for danger signals, 'something's upsetting him now ...'

Rough-knuckled Tom Wilkinson didn't care much for naval niceties. When he'd first taken command he had scandalised visiting VIPs by receiving them in singlet, shorts and slippers. Similarly, on manoeuvres, he had no sooner astonished official observers by sinking three out of six enemy submarines than he'd blotted his copybook by obeying the command 'Return to base' too promptly and taking a short cut across the flagship's bows.

But incidents like these, retailed extensively in the pre-Pearl Harbour days by men consoling themselves over long iced drinks at the club for being kept from the war in Europe, did not count for much among his immediate associates.

Wilkie, they agreed, was a bit of a character. A slave-driving customer with a tongue like a flail. But, as a sailor, the old man was second to none.

For instance, the *Li Wo* had recently rescued all but one of the crew of a sister patrol craft which had been bombed and sunk by the Japanese.

Wilkie had done the job at a time when the enemy aircraft had come in so low that they'd been forced to split formation in order to dodge the funnel ...

'That was something to shout about,' the QM conceded, with unexpected fervour, as he remembered how Wilkinson had threaded the *Li Wo* between the crowded rafts and lifeboats as if he were handling a skiff on a park pond. 'But there's no accounting for his moods. At the moment, he's as miserable as hell.'

Tom Wilkinson returned to life abruptly, shaking himself like a wet dog in his efforts to shrug off his gloomy thoughts.

Pity that the one man he had not been able to save had been the captain ... Pity that the captain, one of his closest friends, had been beheaded by a bomb splinter as cleanly as by a Samurai sword.

Pity, a hell of a pity – but one couldn't mope for

ever. There were the living to consider; one could not help the dead.

Tom Wilkinson strode to the bridge rail, blew his nose like a trumpet and glared malevolently at the working party on the deck below.

'Get a bloody move on, you sods. Don't you know there's a bloody war on?'

Wilkie was on form again.

'An incredible business ... landing in the muck like this.' Neal Derbridge spoke with an almost cheerful detachment.

Stanton looked at the young New Zealander, *Li Wo*'s sole RNVR Sub, like a man who'd just heard the understatement of the year. 'There are stronger words than incredible,' he answered dryly.

An empire had been attacked and overrun. An impregnable fortress had become a crowded trap. The Eastern fleets of the Allies had been destroyed or crippled . . . and all this had happened in the space of sixty-four days.

By now the front was only three miles away. Echoes of the furious conflict came cracking over the anchorage like the sound of a forest fire. On the heights of Pasir Panjang, screening the ships to the north-east, United Kingdom troops and men of the Malay Regiment were fighting to stem the Jap torrent from spilling on to the beaches. The 22nd Australian Brigade – what little was left of it – was locked in hand-to-hand combat in the ruins of Tanglin, the Singapore suburb that lay on the *Li Wo*'s starboard. The Naval Base – top right-hand corner of the diamond-shaped island –

was already by-passed and isolated. To the south, detachments of local volunteers, deploying to guard against invasion from the sea, had found instead the enemy at their backs.

'It's the past fortnight that's proved so damned decisive,' said someone, searching for a reason. 'If it hadn't been for the speed of things over this past fortnight we'd be sitting pretty by now. The land defences could have been strengthened ... the air forces have a chance to build up in Sumatra. The chaps from the peninsular could have rested and re-formed ... and the new chaps from Britain been able to dig their heels in.'

'Or at least get rid of their ruddy winter woollies!'

There was a short silence.

'Poor bloody Pongoes,' said Derbridge sorrowfully. 'Fresh from the English fog. Good material ... the best in the world. And all of them wasted. Chucked into the pan ...'

'And now the ruddy Nips have pulled the chain,' commented Jimmy Murray, *Li Wo*'s chief engineer. But the pawky Scot had not intended to pun. And no one smiled.

There'd been quite a sensation when the 19th Division arrived in Singapore: but it was caused not by hope, but by incredulity. Brought safely from England by the Navy's sacrifice, the 19th was supposed 'to reinforce the island's defences' – but these 'defences' had already ceased to exist. Poor bloody Pongoes, ill-equipped and stiff jointed from their three months' sea trip, they hadn't a hope in hell.

Yet fortune, which had so outrageously tipped the scales against their courage, had been no kinder to their predecessors, the gaunt and fever-ridden men who had reeled over the causeway from Johore.

For these, the veterans who'd survived the horrors of a retreat that had lasted since mid-December and extended for over four hundred and fifty miles, Singapore had seemed, at the time, like the promised land.

Prepared positions, artillery and air support, the vast resources of a fortress … all these, they'd believed, would now be theirs … the reward of bloody sacrifice and torment, the justification for their devoted obedience. A great day indeed, the day they'd crossed the causeway … a day to remember and give thanks for seeing. And then the Japs had swept across the Straits, and the nightmare had reached its hideous climax.

'I wouldn't be a Pongo,' said Murray, 'for all the tea in China.'

'Agreed, agreed, Chiefie, but they can stuff the Navy, too!'

They'd built the *Li Wo* for the Yangtse river trade: her place of birth was Hong Kong.

She was a small ship, a very small ship … the smallest member of the company's Eastern fleet. She was sometimes described as a rather ugly ship, but in commerce looks are not everything. There are virtues that can make up for an unattractive shape, and the *Li Wo* had such virtues. For example, she made a profit.

Her coal-burning engines were gratifyingly economical: they were also surprisingly powerful. She was fast, by river standards, for she could make a good fifteen knots. She was also very manoeuvrable, and had a draught of only eight feet. For a ship designed to negotiate the Upper Gorges of the stiff-flowing Yangtse these things were vital. From the thin armour plate round her bridge, to divert the bullets of river pirates, to the huge Union Jack that, painted on her side, warned Chinese and Japanese of her protected neutrality, the little *Li Wo* had been ideally equipped for the humdrum, but profitable, peace-time role assigned her. Unfortunately, however, she had little time to play it.

Red funnel with black top ... buff hull with distinctive thin blue line ... deck houses in blazing white ... it was difficult, nowadays, to recall her Yangtse livery. But her unromantic structure had not changed.

There was little warlike swank about the steamer. When Stanton, an enthusiast for camouflage, had painted her in a dazzle-scheme of contrasting greys and greens, she had startled some of her witty detractors by coming first in a gunnery exercise. But her victory, like her camouflage, did not seem convincing. HMS *Showboat* was a ship without illusions.

Four days' patrol, two days at Changi Base ... four days' patrol, then four at Changi Base; until Pearl Harbour her wartime beat was as humdrum as the most uneventful Yangtse voyage, and infinitely less useful, or so it had seemed to her multi-racial crew. British, Malay and Chinese, they were as remote from the traditional naval image as the little *Li Wo* herself, or the half-dozen officers who commanded her.

Most of them company men, given temporary commissions, the officers had accepted the war as a necessary evil and were prepared to play their part. But they'd expected that part to be a serious one, justifying being uprooted from a peaceful and lucrative job. Instead, they'd been confronted by long periods of inaction, and their initial enthusiasm had speedily begun to wane. Off-duty they found Singapore expensive: compared with their old haunts on the China Coast it was also damned dull. On-duty their gloom increased; so little seemed to be happening. It was difficult to feel 'hilarious' – the description was Tom Wilkinson's – when doubling for 'real' warships, bound for Europe. For the Japanese were still friendly, and the German enemy stayed half a world away.

Four days' patrol, then two days at Changi Base … four days' patrol, then four at Changi Base … it had been the pattern of their lives as well as the *Li Wo*'s. A pattern they now looked back on with an almost frenzied longing. At the time it had seemed so unbearably dull.

In the West, the 'phoney' war, with all its attendant strains on morale, had lasted for less than eight months. In the East they had been subjected to its subtleties for two years and a quarter. But the blow, when it fell, had come heavier than the blitzkrieg. Only nine weeks had passed since the beginning, yet already they were watching what seemed to be the end.

'Wonder when they'll kindly tell us to go ... get out for good, I mean,' said Neal.

'Don't know,' answered Stanton. 'Can't see we'll be much use. The *Showboat* lacks even ornamental value.'

Pale puffs of smoke expanded in the sky, showering steel splinters around the weaving aircraft. The crew flattened themselves on the deck. The dust displaced by the last bomb, somewhere beyond the power-station behind the coal wharf, rose high above the go-downs, a filthy grey.

'And to think it wasn't so long ago that I was moaning about the lack of excitement,' Neal said. 'Pining to get to the Med ... and that old ship of mine ...'

'You and your ruddy destroyer! You're always talking of her!'

'Well, she was the first I'd served in. And a happy ship, too ...'

'Sure she was – you'll have me crying my ruddy eyes out. What's John Manston doing?'

The *Li Wo*'s 'third' had come hurrying from the bridge towards the gangplank. The note of urgency was not typical.

'Good God,' Stanton exclaimed. 'Done up like a dog's dinner, and in a hurry too. Don't tell us you've actually got a date ashore!'

Manston blew fastidiously at the crisp gold braid on his sleeve. 'But certainly, old chap ... on a diplomatic mission. The thing needs tact, the old man said … and he can trust no one but me.'

'Okay. Now will you put us wise? Will you tell us what's happening?'

'But that,' drawled Manston, 'is what I'm supposed to find out.'

Wilkie had told him sourly: 'Make a report to Fort Canning on the bombing … then ferret out what gives. What the hell do they want us to do? And when the hell can we go? But make it tactful, of course. Wouldn't want those chair-polishers to think we've got the wind up.'

When John had described his mission, Stanton said, 'And the best of British luck. We can do with all we can get …'

To Manston the subsequent journey was confusing, even though it would have been against his habit to show it. The last time he'd made the trip had been in a limousine, chauffeur-driven, with some society women. Manston had done well in Singapore.

But now the guns thundered continuously. From bomb-broken drains arose an overpowering stench. Some streets were so empty that he could hear his footsteps echoing. Others were so full that he had to force his way through the ebbing and flowing mass of confused and frightened people. From the flak-speckled sky the waspish drone of aero engines never seemed to let up.

Aboard the *Li Wo*, John Manston had an almost legendary reputation for loving comfort: he spent his off-duty hours lying in the sun. Yet though the sight of him, spread-eagled in his deck-chair aft the little river steamer's funnel, had more than once affronted orthodox naval men, Wilkinson seldom nagged him. Maybe it was because he could pierce the pose of indolence – for pose it was – and appreciate the real calibre of the man beneath it. Or maybe it was because it was impossible to be seriously annoyed with one who made light of everything that was serious.

Yet, this time, even Manston's ostentatious nonchalance began to slip a little. The sense of doom about the city was contagious, arousing unexpected fear.

At a place where three roads met, he found a small group of Australians, rigging up a machine-gun post. Survivors of the retreat down the Peninsular, they bore the scars of the mauling they'd received: human skeletons, but working hard. Their comments about the treatment they'd give the Japs were unanimous, and blasphemous. Manston, quite fascinated, paused to listen, and admire.

But as he did so he recognised a local European, a successful planter he'd met at a classy party. At the time of their encounter Singapore was at peace: a symbol of Western power and affluence and an oasis of tranquillity. Neither of the men, as they sipped their cocktails, had the remotest suspicion that the place wouldn't stay that way. Quite ignorant of the coming storm – it was to break in four days' time – their conversation had been confined to such prosaic problems as

Christmas shopping. How, for example, could they get the luxury goods available in the city back to relatives at home? But now Manston found his friend in the sweat-stained uniform of a European volunteer. Much thinner, his face heavily lined, he was helping the Aussies to unload sandbags from a truck.

Manston asked, 'How's tricks?'

The planter shrugged. 'Managed to get the kids away, and persuaded the wife to follow them. They're safe by now, or at least I hope so.'

'Good for you,' Manston answered.

'We've lost everything else, though it doesn't matter much now. Come to think of it,' he added, with a twisted smile, 'I don't think that anything's going to matter. Not out here ... not to the West again. We've had it!'

He jerked his head at the lean Australians. 'These chaps are okay. But there's loads of others who aren't. Take a look at some of the Indians – there's no reason why they should worry about us.'

An Aussie NCO interrupted them. 'Hey, there, cobber, you going to yarn all day?'

His voice was not unkind; it belied the heavy sarcasm of the words. His eyes, puckered with crows-feet and smudged with sleeplessness, peered into the officer's: they were questioning. 'Any news from the Navy, mate? We heard a bloody great fleet was on its way ...'

Manston bowed his well-groomed head. 'Sorry, old boy, but they don't tell us very much ...'

'S'all right, cobber. Message understood.'

But there was bitterness in his voice as he quietly added, 'My boys are willing to mix it, but I doubt if they'll be allowed to. This place stinks of defeat. It's lost the will to fight …'

Manston gloomily completed the journey to HQ. Nor did the orders he got there raise his spirits. On the other hand, he reflected, the old man's comments about them should be well worth hearing. Wilkie had a flair for describing the peculiar ways of officialdom. Brightened by this idea, he combed his hair and brushed his tunic; with luck he'd have time to scrounge a large pink gin before setting out on his return trip to the ship.

Wilkinson listened to Manston's short report, then sent for Stanton. 'Ronnie, I've got some news. We've got our orders at long last.'

'Thank Christ,' said Number One.

The skipper smiled sourly. 'I'd rather thank Fort Canning. They say we're to carry on with normal routine patrols. Probably nuts,' Wilkinson added with relish, 'for there's certainly nothing routine about this dump today. But orders are orders.'

'The men's reactions will scarcely be hilarious,' warned Stanton.

'Hilarious? More like a bloody wake. Wouldn't be so bad if they'd a chance of battle. Or thought the old tub was doing anything useful …'

The officers' guess about the unpopularity of HQ's latest orders was accurate. Some of the local inhabitants got out of harm's way, while the Europeans swore like troopers.

For what was the purpose of the *Li Wo*'s assignment? What sort of enemy was she supposed to be looking for? A submarine? Her A/S bomb-blasted to bits, and HQ knew it. Something larger, then? In that case, with one vintage four-incher, it was a damned shame the planners couldn't come along for the trip.

'But it's the poor devils on the wharf that I'm most sorry for,' said Derbridge. Ronald Stanton shrugged, affecting callousness.

The shocked survivors of broken units, the once proud wives of colonial officials, the sick and the wounded – all these, who had been mustering since dawn upon the cold wharf, were pitiable enough. But the sight of the kids was the hardest to bear. For a crowd of destitute children, infected by the panic of the adults, was clamouring on the quayside to be taken away.

'But surely you'll take my child. Surely you wouldn't turn away a child!'

The woman's face was scarlet with weeping. Dirt, strain and sweat disfigured her face. Her expensively bought dress was in shreds and stiffly crusted with dust from the coal dump into which she'd burrowed during the last air raid.

'Please,' she said. 'We've relatives in Batavia.'

The child in her arms was about three years old, and too terrified to cry. It sucked a fat thumb, already red and raw, and stared at them, first at its mother, then at Stanton; lastly it fixed its eyes on Wilkinson, who was overcome by an unusual embarrassment.

'I'm not asking you to take me on your bloody ship,' she said. 'I'm only asking you to take my baby ...'

And she held the child up to him supplicatingly.

'For goodness sake believe me,' he protested, 'we are not going to Batavia. We are going out on patrol. We are going out on a job where all of us may be drowned.'

'My child ... just one small child ... surely you can take my child!'

'You just don't know what you're asking.'

But she would not listen and, on his final refusal, broke into a pitiful tirade of abuse, echoed by other members of the wharfside queue.

'Coward!' she cried. 'And you call yourself an Englishman!'

Wilkie damned her, and turned away. But he was genuinely upset. A tough character, one of the toughest on a beat not much frequented by weaklings, this sort of thing unnerved him, and the howling injustice of it brought him close to tears ... tears of rage. What sort of monkey did they take him for? Nothing would have pleased him better than to have taken the baby on board. God damn it, he'd have run a shuttle service, if need be, for the benefit of those poor devils on the quay. But orders had to be obeyed. The crowd on the wharf just didn't understand. They refused to believe the ship was scheduled for further thankless duty in the approaches to the island. The rumour that she was preparing to go to Java was strong among them, and their shouting grew louder.

Just before the *Li Wo* finished coaling – a lengthy job, for all the local labour had disappeared – two women and their babies were discovered in the fo'c'sle. They had to be put ashore, but the job was heart-breaking.

When the *Li Wo* eventually cast off, to anchor in Keppel Harbour and wait for a sailing time, the jeers came louder than ever from the hopeless crowd.

CHAPTER TWO

A Ship Flees Singapore

Night had fallen, but the darkness was lit by flames of a hundred fires. Stanton, remembering the events of the day, felt mentally and physically crushed. He was too tired and sick even to eat his dinner.

No further instructions had arrived regarding the sailing time. Communications appeared to have broken down. Rumours spread among the crew. Some whispered that the signals station opposite had been abandoned, leaving the ships to fend for themselves. Others, repeating gossip picked up from refugees on the wharfside, said that HQ was now determined to surrender. Only London's disapproval, it was said, stood in the way of capitulation by dawn.

Like summer lightning, a brilliant flash suddenly lit up the sloping face of Blakin Mati, the 'forces' island' that lay to the *Li Wo*'s port and opposite the Singapore shore. And, echoing over the water, the dockland and the low conical hills that closed around the harbour, the thunder followed, the thunder from the batteries crouched among the military bungalows and the scrub.

As the heavy shells screamed over the *Li Wo*, to explode, miles away and out of sight, among the plantations to the north, a cheer arose from the little ship's mixed company. It was an ironic cheer, but not unkindly meant. All the men on the steamer knew by now that the artillery was 'blind'. Or that the most formidable guns of all in terms of calibre were equipped solely with armour-piercing shell next to useless against infantry. But, all the same, it was reassuring to hear the explosions. It was good to know that up at Blakin Mati, despite the inevitable reprisals that would follow, the army was still bloody-minded: still was eager to have a crack at this invisible, yet ever-advancing, enemy.

Wilkinson, watching from the bridge, found particular satisfaction in what he called 'The Crystal Palace Show'.

'Maybe some of the yellow bastards will have copped it good and strong,' he said to Derbridge.

In Murray, the Scots engineer, however, the bombardment aroused deep anxiety.

His brother, a Royal Navy petty officer, had been stationed at Singapore Base … had his home among the hills that now hurled back the echo of the guns. Jimmy had spent many leaves in the trim bungalow there, happy to talk about the old days in Renfrew while drinking cool beer on the veranda or else, carpet-slippered, to be fussed over by his sister-in-law and her family. To Jimmy, not so robust as some of his younger colleagues, such domestic interludes had meant a lot. Though for years a confirmed wanderer, he had come to feel increasingly a need for relaxation and sense of belonging, which only the 'family' could provide. And now? He shivered slightly as he peered into the flame-dashed darkness. He could get no news at all of what had happened to those he loved.

Stanton's voice interrupted his thoughts. 'Penny for them, Jimmy ...' Yet, instinctively, he'd already guessed the reason for the Scot's unusual melancholy, for Stanton, too, had often visited the bungalow with Jimmy.

'They were darn good to me, Ronnie,' Murray said simply. 'And I'm scared ... dead scared ... that we'll never meet them again.'

There were tears in his eyes as he went abruptly below.

Stanton, his depression increased by the brief exchange, did not stay on deck for long. He knew that he'd need all the energy he could muster for the day ahead. When he entered his cabin he put his head down at once. And then, flaked out, dropped into a dead sleep.

'Captain wants you, sir.' Stanton glanced blearily at his watch. Two in the morning. After the heat of the day and the stuffiness of the blacked-out cabin, the air seemed unnaturally cold, and he shivered as he passed the gun crew to join the dark bulk of Wilkinson, motionless near the wheel.

Ronald George Stanton, aged thirty-two, was a short, tough man. He could draw on vast reserves of seamanlike cunning when coping with the eccentricities of the ocean but, being a man of peace, he didn't like assuming a military role.

'Besides, I don't really belong to this war of yours,' he'd used to joke in the days before Pearl Harbour. 'I'm just not interested. I'm a neutral.'

This was, of course, untrue, and designed to tease. Ronnie was as British as they come, and had shown a natural bent for picking up the Navy's tricks of war. But the 'neutral' line dated from the time when he'd first joined the ship and Wilkinson had welcomed him aboard. 'Damned glad to see you,' the latter had exclaimed. 'It's not every day we see a bloody Yankee come to help in the war.'

It was useless, after that, for Stanton to try to explain that he'd spent his leaves in the United States merely because his parents had happened to emigrate there and because his girl lived there. Useless to protest he was British-born and a Northerner to the core. Once Wilkinson had made up his mind there was no point in trying to change it. True that officially Stanton had UK status, but Wilkie thought he knew better, trusting his intuition. 'Thank God,' he'd exclaimed to the Yankee warmly, after news of Pearl Harbour's ordeal, 'thank God that at last we're all in this together!'

It was no time to think about flag distinctions. 'Just got our sailing time; it's immediate,' Wilkinson growled. 'But where the hell's the carpenter?'

The *Li Wo*'s carpenter was an expert getter-up of anchors. Today, however, it was impossible to find him.

'Very sorry,' said one of the few Chinese still on board. 'Johnnie, he go along shoreside. He got wife and child along shoreside. He scarper, sir …'

'Well, isn't that too bad,' said Wilkinson. 'I'll chop the next bastard who tries to do a bunk.'

Yet to Stanton he added with surprising charity: 'Can't blame 'em really. It's our mess, Ronnie.'

Despite her short-handedness, the *Li Wo* managed to weigh by 0220. But soon she found herself inching through a man-made smog, a smog that had crept from the shore during the ordeals of the night. Originally Tom Wilkinson had aimed at making an immediate passage to the sea by way of Keppel Harbour, but as soon as the ship had cleared the head he found that his plans had been unduly optimistic. The smoke was thicker than ever, worse than a London fog. Somehow or other, 'by guess and by God', they managed to reach Examination Anchorage – the customs area outside the harbour – but they could proceed no farther. Visibility was almost nil.

For a while Wilkinson waited, scowling into the fog as though attempting to browbeat it into dispersal. But nothing short of a gale could budge this curtain of greenish-grey. The ship must stay in the area until daybreak. There was no help for it. He decided to hand over to Stanton.

'I'm proper done in,' he confessed with unusual candour, 'and I mustn't be caught napping when we get our morning caller.'

As the captain turned away from the bridge the weight of long accumulated sleeplessness overtook him, dragging his legs and bowing his broad shoulders. There was a limit to even Wilkinson's endurance, and that limit had now been reached.

'Poor bastard,' thought Stanton. 'No rest but catnaps ... not for a ruddy week!'

The sea was dead calm, but the air was tormented by the noise of battle. There was no horizon, no visible meeting-place between the waters and the sky. Even the fringe of the *Li Wo*'s lazy wake was hardly discernible. The setting was uncanny, stranger than anything the watch had yet encountered. When the fog lifted they could catch brief glimpses of Keppel Harbour ... or the grey shadow of the examination steamer, lit up by the glare of burning oil tanks. But the periods of visibility were fleeting and lasted only so long as fierce gusts of wind and flame combined to combat the foul-smelling smoke that had blacked-out the anchorage and wrapped round the *Li Wo*. The position of the ship was, to say the least, unenviable. A minefield, designed to protect the island from seaborne assault, lay south of them: there was a reef to the north. Constant watchfulness was essential, yet this was almost impossible to maintain after the long days and nights of strain. Sleep crept like a traitor to the bridge, caressing the tired eyes of the occupants and, with the smoke an ally, smothering their brains. It was difficult to resist such insidious advances, and each, though repelled, laid fresh stresses on the overtaxed defenders.

The dawn of February 12th brought relief to the men of the *Li Wo* and they forgot the danger of their situation. Stiff bodies stretched out and eased in the early daylight. Their spirits temporarily rose.

By 0650 the *Showboat*, her tattered White Ensign flying from the mast, was back on the old familiar beat.

Searching for God-knew-what, she steamed to and fro, her capacity to manoeuvre restricted by the jagged reefs that formed the boundaries of the patrol area; she was a slow-moving toy to the Japanese bomb-aimers.

'Shoot!' Neal Derbridge's voice was unwontedly shrill. 'Shoot!' And the four-inch gun hurled its angry missile through the sky.

But Wilkinson had no time to see whether it had reached its target. And the motion of the *Li Wo*, recoiling from the firing, was a bad sign of the effectiveness for the gun crew. As an anti-aircraft weapon the *Li Wo*'s four-incher, with a maximum elevation of only thirty-five degrees, had always been a dead loss. But flak action now, swore Neal, was hopeless.

The first wave of bombers came in at two hundred feet. Wilkinson tensed himself.

He had watched the progress of these planes from the moment of their appearance to the moment when they peeled off from the main formation. In a few minutes he had seen them changed from silvery works of beauty into raucous monsters threatening to smash his ship to matchwood. 'But damn you,' he cried aloud. 'I'll show you a trick or two yet.'

He now proceeded to make his boast come true. The spokes of the wheel spun in blurred haste beneath the fingers of the duty QM.

The three propellers, designed to give the ship manoeuvrability in the treacherous Yangtse gorges, carried the *Li Wo* in a crazy slithering dance. The leading Japanese plane dropped a stick of bombs: they missed. Again Wilkinson directed his ship along a swiftly changing course, and again the bombs fell wide. Then the machine-guns fired furiously, presenting the enemy with added confusion. Wilkie grinned purposefully.

Stanton had little time to study the behaviour of his captain. But now Wilkinson was like a man transformed.

His face upturned, intent on estimating the moment of the bombs' departure, he was a picture of tough assurance, a man whose brain, body and commanding voice formed a flawlessly operating human machine.

Li Wo responded to him like a thoroughbred to a master rider's touch. At one moment of crisis she heeled over on her side, but only to skid across the surface of the water in a sort of hide-and-seek between the showering bomb-bursts. In another attack it seemed that she was spinning like a top.

But the Japanese still came on, more furiously than ever.

The helmsman was hurled across the planks by the blast. The wheel spun madly and, as Stanton tried to steady it, yet another near-miss sent a hail of iron across the bridge and a cascade of filthy water into the tilting scuppers. Almost as soon as the *Li Wo* recovered from the assault, the Malay was at his post again. 'You give me back wheel, sir.'

'All right, take it easy; no one's trying to rob you!'
'Strike a light!' exclaimed Mac in rich Australian accents. 'Now there's a regular Gunga Din!'

'The good ones are like that,' panted Stanton. 'Now let's get cracking.'

'Cobber, you should have seen some of the bastards we had to put up with!'

'Enough of that. We've other things to think of!' Mac was a Wilkinson discovery. An Australian, he'd caught the skipper's eye by the way in which, jettisoning his own personal worries, he'd lent a willing hand helping on the coal wharf when the crew were bunkering the ship. His energy and bawdy cheerfulness had made a deep impression on Wilkinson, always a shrewd acquisitor of whatever might be useful to the *Showboat*. Just before she cast off Mac had been told to jump aboard and get signed on for 'general utility purposes'. Such a method of recruitment was, of course, unorthodox … and typical of Wilkinson. But Stanton now had good reason to congratulate the skipper on his choice.

Although no bomb had hit the ship, the effect of the near-misses was sufficiently alarming. All over the wooden deck, timber-dry in the sun, the little flames began to flicker. They stamped on them, then put out the fire in the wreckage of the chief's cabin. Another burst of bombs, and they dived for the wheelhouse.

A large fragment of metal cut through the deckhead on to the top bridge.

'Jeeze …!' exclaimed the Australian. 'A second earlier and you'd have been the target!'

'Don't talk about it,' said Stanton, feeling suddenly ill.

More Japanese planes came roaring in, their bullets ripping through the upper deck. Once more there was the whine of bombs, the evil stench of explosives griped the stomachs of the deck crew. Rearing abruptly from the green-blue sea, columns of writhing yellow water hovered above the little ship and then overbalanced, collapsing harmlessly into the churned-up spume.

It was the last assault. The aircraft's strident clamour receded slowly. The *Showboat*, under the guidance of Tom Wilkinson, had reached the protection of the guns: the AA batteries that blazed from Keppel Head.

Silence fell completely, almost eerily. As the ship lost way, Wilkinson, his hands still clasping the bridge rail, stared blankly at the shell-torn hillock for a few minutes, and then turned to examine the damage on the deck below. 'They've made a ruddy mess of our glasswork. Number One,' he bawled. 'A round of inspection, if you please!'

There were almost a hundred holes in the ship's sides, ranging from gashes as large as a man's head to neat little punctures smaller than a baby's fist. The funnel, riddled by splinters, resembled a pepper-pot. The cabins on the upper deck were gutted. Below, where Stanton had built shelters for the Chinese, hysteria was rife. He was told that someone was lying wounded in the aft latrine, but none of the Chinese would accompany him on the work of rescue ...

It was Rajah, the Malay signalman. The top of his head had been blown off, but he was alive, although unconscious. He lay in a space about two feet wide, and the lieutenant had difficulty in getting him out.

Another Singapore night ... but the *Li Wo*'s Europeans, despite hours spent in shovelling smashed glass and woodwork over the ship's side, were relatively high-spirited. Tom Wilkinson had at last been told that the ship could prepare to leave for Batavia, possibly with passengers. The buzz had got round.

Food came aboard, 'requisitioned' from abandoned go-downs by Robertson, a plump and genial former company captain. Fresh reinforcements arrived, among them Royal Navy regulars. Despite the knowledge of the impending disaster on the island, and an awareness of the dangers of the voyage, there was a mild sense of celebration amongst the company.

At 5 p.m., with the ship ready for sea, the officers foregathered for a drink, and Mac, living up to his reputation for usefulness, produced a surprise feature – a really excellent meal. To do this he had to act as cook and steward combined: the local boys who usually did the job still keeping to their hiding-places, too terrified to move. Conjectures regarding their present activities were lewd but good-natured, no one having the heart to boot them back to duty.

It was, in fact, an almost jolly affair, this farewell party aboard the little steamer that tomorrow, should she live that long, would start to run the merciless gauntlet of the omnipresent Japanese. Everyone exhibited ostentatiously high spirits. Everyone seemed determined to show up at his best. Yet the gaiety was forced, born of desperation. Certainly the *Li Wo*'s officers had few illusions regarding the difficulties of the voyage. The way through the narrow channels, which culminated in the bottleneck of Banka Strait, was a lot more hazardous now than it had been three days before. The bodies of men, women and children, yesterday's would-be refugees, were washed up by the oil-cloaked waters of each tide on to the beaches of the island and the lush-green fringes of neighbouring Sumatra.

And even now, though starved of official guidance, the men of the *Li Wo* could sense the movements of their constantly active foe. His right fist would be sweeping southward from the Gulf of Siam. His left would be travelling westward from his new-won base in Borneo. And both blows would be aimed at the very heart of the territory in which the steamer was seeking refuge.

And yet, it was a comparatively pleasant evening. Only when they came on deck did the officers fall silent, and consider ...

The tropical night had pulled its vast black blind across the troubled sky. The Japanese bombers had long since left for home, but a necklace of flames was looped around the shore. Fires were burning everywhere, and the roar of them was carried on the wind. Occasionally the silent watchers would see a launch or sampan leave her moorings crowded with refugees, and scurry along the edges of the channel, dodging the flares and searchlights. But the flights became more infrequent as the night progressed.

The coastal batteries continued to thunder from across the harbour, but only with the purpose of unloading their ammunition in an impressive last fling. At times the distinctive crackle of rifle fire rose to a fierce crescendo.

The Japanese had pierced the southern defence lines; had now almost reached the shore.

At midnight Stanton went below again. He chatted with Jimmy Murray, the chief engineer, still worried stiff about his brother's family, and with John Manston, the *Li Wo*'s debonair third.

And then, as they were talking about their chances, Neal Derbridge dropped in to say, unexpectedly, 'It's God's will that will decide.'

'But, damn it, Neal.' Manston's normal drawl was transformed into a high-pitched exclamation of surprise. 'Don't tell us that you're religious.'

Neal Derbridge glanced away. 'Why, he's blushing,' retorted Stanton. 'Actually blushing.'

But the New Zealander's reply was defiant. 'If you mean by religious that I believe in God, you're right. Whatever happens will be His will.'

'Oh, sorry. Didn't mean to offend.'

Silence followed, broken only by the dull echoes from the shore.

'Nice young chap that,' said Murray, as Derbridge left for the bridge. 'Hell of a nice fellow.'

'Agreed, Chiefie, agreed. Too good for this ruddy business.'

More silence.

Somehow the knowledge that Neal – so 'normal' and popular – should hold more than professional convictions embarrassed them. Every member of the crew had been praying hard recently, but they'd kept the fact to themselves.

'Bloody lot of inverted hypocrites, that's what we are!' exclaimed Manston suddenly.

'Hypocrites?'

'Oh, damn it. You know what I mean. We've all of us – yes, all of us – run whining to God in the past few days, but we haven't the guts to confess it. Not in public. Might make us look scared, old chap. And that would be unforgivable.'

'You've got something,' reflected Stanton, reaching for a gin. 'You've really got something. In a sense, I suppose, we could be called the cabin-class Christians: the ones who want privileges, but without the responsibility. We trust, instinctively, the ship, without ever helping to work it. And when in difficulties, we reach for the nearest bell.'

An ominous darkness and silence rested over Fort Canning. There were now only four ships remaining in the harbour and the senior captain had been signalling for hours for orders, without result.

At 2.15 a.m. he made one last effort, using both lights and wireless, but there was still no reply. He decided that it was his duty to carry out the verbal instructions issued earlier, and which the signals were to have confirmed.

At 2.20 a.m. the little convoy at last got under way. It was Friday – Friday the 13th.

CHAPTER THREE

Friday The 13th

Stanton, in a brief visit to his cabin, placed his girl's picture face downwards under his pillow.

Next, tacitly conforming to respectable naval tradition, he changed into clean vest and pants. He didn't give much for the *Li Wo*'s chances: and felt if he had to die, he might as well die decent.

Ronald Stanton was not usually a pessimist, but he had few illusions about the dangers of the escape route. The South China Sea had become a Japanese lake. To get to Batavia, her nearest refuge, the little ship must run the enemy gauntlet for seven hundred miles.

As he reported back to the bridge, Stanton wryly recalled the blasphemous 'Grace' of Nelson's men: 'For what we are about to receive, may the good Lord make us truly thankful.'

It seemed appropriate to the *Li Wo*'s prospects.

Impatience and anger marked the beginning of the odyssey.

Wilkinson, after the desertions at the coal wharf, had promised the Asians that they would be free to go before the ship left Singapore, but the exercise was bedevilled from the start. First, when he asked for the names of those who wished to leave, nearly every Asian had stepped smartly forward – 'a bit of a facer,' as he'd ruefully conceded. Next, when the ship received her sailing orders she was lying in midstream, and a boat could not be spared.

Yet to write off his promise was not in the nature of Tom Wilkinson – stubborn, dogmatic, priding himself on his word.

So, to the annoyance of the impatient Europeans, he interrupted the ship's passage out of harbour and steered towards a moored lighter, to transfer those who wished to leave the ship.

'With luck,' he said, 'they can get ashore in the morning.'

This strangely quixotic gesture had all the odds against it. The lighter, unmanned, was rolling heavily. The *Li Wo* managed to close her, but in the heavy swell it was difficult to keep her alongside when only using the engines. But the biggest obstacle to Wilkinson's plan succeeding lay in the behaviour of those it had been designed to help.

Hitherto almost hysterically vocal about their desire to leave the ship, the vast majority showed marked reluctance to risk their lives by jumping. Frightened to stay with the ship, they were even more frightened to go.

'I'll give you ten minutes,' Wilkinson bawled. 'And after that I'll have to pull away …'

But his warning had little effect.

When the *Li Wo* eventually backed away, her self-appointed task was less than half complete.

And the rest of the little convoy was far ahead, and out of sight.

Comment among the Europeans was almost universal: so the Wogs hadn't made it? Too bloody bad!

Only Derbridge, the New Zealander, displayed a different view. 'Poor devils,' he argued. 'This war isn't really their business.'

'You're a nice chap, Neal, and I'd hate to quarrel with you,' commented a colleague quietly. 'But could you tell me what business it is of ours?'

Stanton broke a rather unpleasant silence.

'This old tub's not making her usual knots,' he said. 'Murray must be in difficulty with the stokers.'

Jimmy Murray, chucking aside his gauntlets, grabbed the tin mug with a greedy self-conscious gesture, as though half-disgusted with himself. First, he rinsed his mouth with the tepid water, spitting out the cloying coal-dust and turning it into a hissing steam on the burning plates of the catwalk. Next, he drank deeply, appreciatively, smacking his lips before heaving a gentle sigh of melancholy and gratitude, like an old man seeking sleep.

And then, with no insignia of rank save the battered officer's cap perched on the back of his black-encrusted head, he again bent his thin body over a shovel and turned his face towards the fire.

For a chief to do a fireman's job was revolutionary, to say the least. 'But if I don't do it,' he'd bleakly informed Wilkinson, 'then no one else will. The men know damn all about it!'

All but two of the Asian firemen had left the ship, and someone had boobed badly in choosing European replacements.

The stoker ratings sent to the *Li Wo* were products of the oil age. They hardly knew how to shovel, much less to rake or slice. To them a stokehole was antiquated, as unfamiliar as the topgallants of a clipper. The ship would never have left her moorings if Murray hadn't show his know-how.

But now, as the shovel resumed its rasping and clanging rhythm, the chief's mind was filled with more than the technical problems of the voyage and his nerves were racked by more than physical distress.

Before coming below he had gazed longingly once more towards the shore, trying to pinpoint his brother's bungalow, the place where he had so often been welcomed. But all he had seen was the glare of the burning – a yellow and red blaze, repetitive each time the furnace door clanged open …

'Sir. I can't stand it!'

Murray, his dreams disturbed, wheeled on the young rating and answered harshly: 'Laddie, you've got to stand it.'

'But, sir …'

'Get a bloody move on,' the normally gentle Scot flared.

Yet as the sobbing youth dragged himself back to work, Murray's eyes held a sort of reluctant compassion.

The *Li Wo*'s lot, abnormal by any standard, would have tried even the most experienced black gangs. But these men were not only strangers to the heat and the back-breaking job below, they were haunted by recent memories of defeat and death. In the depths of the drowning battleships they had seen their comrades die. And now, once again, they were close to death.

'But whatever the snags,' vowed Murray, 'the old tub's got to have steam. Our lives depend on it!'

Up top, as well as below, Friday the 13th continued true to form.

Fresh gusts of foul-smelling smoke, blowing from the burning shore, encircled the *Li Wo*. The blackness was so intense that they'd spotted a white-painted channel buoy only when it was within six feet of tangling with the hull.

And now, tearing aside the fog, came the black hulk of a ship. A ship at speed. On course for head-on collision.

A chorus of shouts, the jangling of the telegraph – as the *Li Wo* lurched violently to port, the horrified officers had a split-second impression of the newcomer's bows breaking through the white curves of foam.

She was rushing at the river steamer like an axe at the chopping block.

Someone yelled, 'We've had it!'

Stanton's brain registered, 'She'll carve us in two!'

And then, astonishingly, the incident was over.

The two ships passed each other with only yards

to spare, and lost each other once more in the blind darkness.

It was Wilkinson who broke the ensuing silence. 'Brave bastard, that, going in to Singapore.'

'Gunboat, Grasshopper class,' commented Stanton shakily. 'Though what good she can do there ...'

Said Ginger Thompson at the wheel, 'I wouldn't be aboard her for a bloody admiral's pension!'

It was with painful slowness that the *Li Wo* continued on her way. The other ships of the convoy did not show up and Wilkinson dared not signal them: Japanese submarines were said to be active locally. Visibility was poor, and finally, off the Raffles light-house – its lamp long since extinguished and its red-and-white striped column invisible in the darkness the ship was forced to anchor.

This further delay tried everyone's patience to excess, but it was Hobson's choice, said Wilkinson. True that daylight would bring in enemy bombers, but there was no hope at all of negotiating the minefield in the dark. They'd just have to like it, or lump it.

The sky paled suddenly, as though a brush had been swept across it, sweeping the blackness into grey. On the bridge they felt the faint cool breath of a breeze: it died in its infancy.

The sun swept savagely above the ocean's rim – a dazzling red ball, and as hateful to the suddenly naked ship as the nation which had adopted it as its symbol.

Ashore, the night noises of the jungle would be giving place to the scream of gaily coloured birds and the chatter of monkeys. Spent bullets would flop amid the English lawns of gutted bungalows. Once more the bomb-shattered drains of Singapore would be throwing up their nauseous fever-laden mist.

But afloat, in this fragile thing of wood and steel, the tensed men's thoughts were of the ocean and the sky. All hands were at action stations. Someone was whistling tunelessly the first bars of a 'pop' song, picked up at a Singapore club. With irony, someone else was humming 'Hearts of Oak'.

On the bridge Lieut. Robertson, seconded to the *Showboat* when his own ship was sunk, was watching for aircraft. As he chain-smoked, a litter of cigarette stubs formed around his feet, drawing mock rebuke from Derbridge. Thompson, his face expressive of nothing but professional aplomb, stood casually, feet astride, beside the wheel. An ex-*Repulse* man, and one of the very few aboard to understand such practical details as the working of a steam windlass, he'd been appointed QM for the voyage's duration: and was settling in nicely thank you. Wilkinson moved to the top bridge, where he remained unusually quiet.

The *Li Wo* had at last regained contact with her sisters, but with two of them only; the third was missing. The buzz had got round that she'd returned to Singapore. But no one knew why, and Wilkinson didn't much care. His thoughts were focused on problems nearer home.

Astonishingly, the senior ship – the ex-company *Fuh Wo* – had not been supplied with charts of the escape route. As a result of this inexplicable omission, *Li Wo* must act as a guide.

'Ronnie,' growled Wilkinson, almost apologetically, 'you're navigator here. I'm afraid it's all your pigeon.'

'And God bless us everyone said Tiny Tim,' reflected Stanton sombrely.

The minefield defending Singapore from the sea was ten miles deep. Its swept channel was somewhat less than three cables wide ... a death-bordered lane in which the ships, deprived of sea room, would be sitting ducks for the Japanese bombs.

Yet to rush things could be equally disastrous. The northern approach buoy, 'signpost' to the lane, had mysteriously vanished. The southern buoy was four cables out of position. A strong easterly sea prevailed, and would necessitate frequent changes of course to hold the ship steady in the channel's (estimated) centre.

As Stanton worried over his navigational plans, John Manston said equably, 'Don't take the worry too personally, old chap. Remember the saying – we're all in the same boat.'

A few minutes later, as the ships edged into the swept channel, the air-raid warning sounded.

Butterflies gyrated in Stanton's stomach: he wanted to spew. With mines a few feet away on either side, and a score of glistening bombers overhead, the *Li Wo*'s survival prospects looked as unpromising as those of a snowball in hell.

Yet, for the moment, fortune was their friend. The Japanese squadrons were hastening to Singapore's kill.

'And to think,' exclaimed Mac, the Australian, bitterly, as plane after plane flew towards the vast pillars of smoke blowing out from the shore, 'that they once said these bastards, these little yellow sons of whores, weren't capable of flying aircraft. They were goggle-eyed, or some darn silly medical term for the same thing ...'

'Myopic,' supplied Number One.

'That's it. Myopic!' repeated Mac admiringly. 'Now how in hell did you know that?'

'Maybe,' said Stanton, with warm eloquence, 'it was the same criminal lunatic who gave us the same illusions. I only wish he, and the rest of the idiot gang, were with us now.'

'With us?' – a horse laugh – 'Cor ... what a ruddy treat!'

Considering the snags, they made the minefield journey pretty smartish. At the time, however, it seemed to take several years. A swing either way could have brought destruction. When the ships passed the buoy marking the channel's exit, Stanton's face was running with sweat.

The *Li Wo* and *Fuh Wo* were now on their own, the sweeper having been ordered to proceed on a separate course. They had all been sorry to see her go, for, as Wilkinson put it, 'misery likes company', but had wasted no time in long drawn-out farewells.

In the meanwhile, with the Japanese aircraft still preoccupied with Singapore, signposted by an ironic Victor-V of smoke, it was decided to get the newcomers better acquainted with the ship; a chore that made Stanton even wearier.

There was so much to do that he'd had no chance of doing before, even such routine as contacting the intake's senior petty officer, CPO Rogers, and sorting the men into their proper watches. With so many Asians remaining, there were feeding and accommodation problems to iron out – not always to everyone's satisfaction. Gun crews, A/S crews, serial look-outs, all had to be organised from scratch.

But the most vital task was to ensure that the coal in the *Li Wo*'s deep tanks reached the stokehold. This was top-grade Welsh, acquired unofficially in the dockside confusion, which made little smoke and could give extra boost to the steam pressure, now fallen from a normal 250 lb to a minimum 110.

Murray, however, had been forced to make fresh demands upon the deck-crew for extra staff to man the furnaces. He needed three times as many hands as he would normally have required had skilled Chinese been available. But this, in turn, meant a reduction in the numbers available for coal-shifting, and even harder work on the part of those remaining. And not all of them saw the need for their exacting task. Tired, disgruntled, and with their prejudices affronted, they sent a deputation to lodge a complaint.

Stanton's initial reactions were coarse, and to the point. But it was only after he'd controlled his temper that he got the effort he wanted.

'In battle every one of these matelots would give the last drop of his blood,' he later confided to Derbridge, 'yet, ask him to do a job that's beneath his status and there's none so restrictionist as your regular British sailor.'

'Maybe it's being so cussed as keeps him, at heart, so good.'

Already Neal had come up against the caste-consciousness of the professional.

Among the regulars was one highly experienced and worthy leading hand. The snag was that Authority, in its wisdom, had allotted him a role far below his natural talents. For the leading hand was a specialist with a passion for torpedoes. And the *Li Wo* had neither torpedoes to fire, nor the tubes from which to fire them. It was like Hamlet without the ghost.

When the news was first broken to him of the little ship's deficiencies, the leading hand's attitude was one of incredulity.

'But what happens if we meet the Nips, sir? What do we hit 'em with?'

'Oh,' answered Neal. 'We'll have to rely on the gun.'

'That.' (immensely scathing) 'But I see it's been made in Tokyo!'

'So is the stuff the other chap will be using!'

The leading hand failed to respond to the joke. Dejectedly his eyes strayed over the *Li Wo*'s ample curves and the square windows of the passenger cabins framed by chintz curtains, incongruously dainty against the jagged bomb-splintered glass.

'Not very much like a real warship, sir. Not quite what one's been used to. A bit Fred Karnoish, if you get what I mean, sir.'

It was only when he heard of Neal's previous appointment, and realised the Subbie had served in a fleet destroyer, that the expert relaxed his professional hauteur. A destroyer man, and reduced to this ... Could there be any greater come-down?

From now on, Neal Derbridge would have his support – and sympathy.

1.30 p.m. ... and the lull was over.

Twenty-six black dots speckled the face of the sun.

'It's us they're coming for this time,' said Wilkinson. 'Us, and us alone. I can feel it in my bones.'

The Japanese approach, made by men who felt themselves secure in godlike inviolability, possessed a certain belligerent majesty. It would have been nonsensical had the *Li Wo* and her sister owned anything more lethal than a low-angle four-inch gun. But, of course, they didn't – and the Japanese seemed to know it. The bombers were flying in a contemptuously neat formation, as if at a peacetime air show. Their leisurely parade offended Thompson. It was, he complained, as if the sky belonged to them. Which, maybe, it did.

Watching them through his field glasses from one wing of the bridge, Tom Wilkinson called to

Stanton, installed in the other, 'I'd give my right hand for a bloody AA gun.'

Then, easing his body outwards from beneath the canvas awning, he forecast, 'They'll be giving us a display of their pattern bombing next.' He was right.

As soon as they saw the Japanese approach, the little ships had changed course, scurrying away from each other in order to get sea room and divide the target. Their only hope lay in their capacity to manoeuvre: they intended to make the most of it. Best drill for the defence, said Wilkinson, drawing freely on experience, would be to watch for the fall of the bombs, guess at their point of impact, and then swing the ship hard away to confuse the bomb aimers. Once more the *Li Wo* began her eccentric dance act.

The bricks were more than usually impressive. Crackling columns of water soared high above the ship. The noise was deafening. At the start Stanton had made a point of throwing himself on the deck, timing this to precede by seconds the showering violence of each bomb-burst. But, after a while, he decided to change his tactics. It wasn't that he'd become over-confident: it was merely because he felt that he was defeating his own purpose of self-preservation.

He discovered this when, having waited in vain for a particularly large missile to explode, he decided it was a dud. And, of course, it wasn't. He had scarcely got to his feet when the bloody thing blew up. It sent a razor-sharp slice of metal into the place where he'd been lying. There was no more flopping.

For the rest of the attack Stanton felt more excited than alarmed. The time was passed in disorganised activity, with Wilkinson and he dashing continually from one side of the bridge to the other, spotting the bombs as they detached themselves from the aircraft, and shouting directions to the helmsman. It was hot work, and confusing: but once more the old man's wild manoeuvring paid off. Most of the Japanese missiles fell well away to the *Li Wo*'s quarter, and even the near-misses did only superficial damage. Each time the bombs came down, the ship tilted over at an alarming angle, plunging off course with such violence that the less acclimatised of her company were swept off their feet. And each time the *Li Wo* bounced out, unscathed, from the seething waters, Wilkie made a vulgar sign with his fingers to the planes above, shouting coarse gibes at their frustrated pilots, as if they could see and hear him.

When the Japanese attack eventually ended, the entire ship's company was seconding the skipper's derisive performance. Yet the ending of the first attack presaged the beginning of another, for the original formation only just turned for base when more bombers appeared. Again there were twenty-six of them, and again they flew high. Again the *Li Wo* went into her St Vitus dance, and again she came out unharmed. But her sister ship was not so fortunate.

Maybe because she was not camouflaged, and so was easier to detect, the Japs concentrated their efforts on her. From *Li Wo* they saw a myriad near-misses splash around her hull, the smoke of two or three hits puff out from her superstructure. And then ... a high-rearing wall rose around her, cutting her off from view.

By the time the attack was over, the *Li Wo*, with waters streaming around her bows like white and green pennants caught by the lash of a gale, had been at action stations for slightly more than two hours. Literally hundreds of bombs had been expended on her as she carved her zigzag pattern of confusion across the once placid sea. And yet this costly bombardment had been totally useless. But there was no trace of her companion: the *Fuh Wo* seemed to have vanished for good. When Wilkinson steered towards the place where she had last been seen it was with the objective of looking for survivors, but the search was fruitless. On the now still water there was no sign of life, riot even a trace of wreckage.

'They've gone for good,' said Wilkie.

A funereal mood descended.

It was half an hour later when, smudging the outline of a nearby island, the look-outs spotted a tell-tale blob of smoke.

Though tremendously battered, the *Fuh Wo* was still afloat. She had found refuge in a bay, where she lay close to the beach.

And there, it transpired, her crew had been mourning the *Showboat!*

The ships were company veterans. Their captains were company cronies. And each had thought the other was a goner.

Small wonder the reunion was an emotional affair, even though Wilkinson and the *Fuh Wo*'s Lieutenant Cook had no illusions about the hazards of the future. With the enemy aircraft as thick as flies, they decided it would be best for the ships to steam under cover of darkness and lie up during the day among the islands. On the other hand, the navigational perils inherent in a night passage would be only a shade less formidable than the danger it was designed to avert. Blacked-out, and with only one set of charts between them, the ships would have to thread their way cautiously through notoriously treacherous waters. For nearly 150 miles their route would lie along shallow, winding channels, far from the main trade routes. And afterwards, at the tip of Sumatra's island-studded shore, they would have to tackle the Banka Strait – a bottleneck completely dominated by the Japanese, and already the graveyard of thousands of Singapore fugitives.

Both commanders were agreed on the great danger of the voyage. Yet the happy coincidence of their meeting served in itself to create a degree of optimism. It was very good to be safe together again. And surely they had not come so far to be pipped at the ruddy post.

Due to the careful timing required to get the ships to a jumping-off point from which they could tackle the Banka and its approaches during the following night, the first lap of the voyage was to be comparatively short. Made in the pre-dawn darkness, with luck it would be completed before the Japs got down to breakfast.

It was 4 p.m. when the conference broke up. The ships were not due to weigh for another eleven hours. Stanton, shelving his problems as navigator, decided to get some sleep.

It was to be his first real sleep for three and a half days, his last real sleep for nearly three and a half years.

Gliding like ghosts between the countless islands, the little ships succeeded in covering fifty miles.

At daybreak they dropped anchor off the coast of Singkep. Here, they hoped, they might be undisturbed until darkness fell again. And in the meanwhile they might as well stop worrying, Wilkinson said. Singkep was as good a hiding place as any. They'd no better place to go ...

It was a brilliant morning. The conical hills were bathed in glaring sunshine. The anchorage was well screened from the seaward side. They thought that from the air the *Li Wo*'s camouflage would blend well with the surrounding colour scheme. Vivid greens and greys of bush and tree, fringing a silver beach.

By 9.50 a.m. the Singkep scene had lost none of its tranquillity. Strained nerves relaxed. Cook was returning to his ship after further conference with Wilkinson. Jimmy Murray had long since let the steam back. The only disturbance on the *Li Wo* came from the unfortunate working party, resuming their job of coal-shifting.

To Ronald Stanton the silence of the island was particularly welcome. His responsibility for the voyage had imposed a hell of a strain. The route had been exceptionally difficult to navigate. But now he could feel pleased at his accurate steering. With luck, he reflected, the day would be restful.

Yet, in hoping for this, he realised he might be tempting providence too far ...

Two aircraft came over the top of the nearest hill – Jap recce planes.

They circled the anchorage, then dived to the attack.

'We've been caught with our pants down,' the SBA exclaimed.

His words were drowned by the scream of falling bombs.

The first almost upset the boat that was carrying Lt Cook back to the *Fuh Wo*.

The next sent a terrible shudder through the length of the *Li Wo*.

CHAPTER FOUR

Enemy Fleet Ahead!

This time, even Wilkinson lost some of his assurance. He rang hard on the telegraph, but the ship couldn't move. The stokers didn't know how to get the fires away quickly; the deck crew didn't know how to work the windlass.

Another near miss, and Neal was alone on the gun platform. The jaded crew had scattered, some throwing themselves in the scuppers.

For a moment panic set in.

As Wilkinson screamed at the gunners to get back to their station, two stokers, deserting Murray, fled for the main-deck. Stanton cursed the windlass … promptly abandoned it … dashed off to give Neal support at the gun. The situation was ugly. The men had long since been tried beyond all the normal limits of endurance: this looked like breaking point.

Yet the crisis ended as quickly as it had begun. It ended unexpectedly, on a note of anti-climax, with the gun crew rallying sheepish and ashamed.

Neal was so busy at the gun that he didn't even curse them. Wilkinson's face went purple, and his hard lips tightened. Stanton, who had helped load and elevate the four-incher, jumped back to the fo'c'sle to hurry up the windlass. 'Too late, though,' he thought 'They're coming in for the kill!'

The gathering roar of the aeroplanes drowned the creaking of the anchor-chain.

This time the Japs approached from starboard. Neal didn't fire. They were flying abreast, and in a shallow dive ... at an angle, he calculated, of about thirty-five degrees. By chance this coincided with the veteran weapon's maximum elevation. So, maybe with luck ... ?

Coolly he waited until they were only three hundred yards away. And then he let fly.

The shell burst midway between the aircraft, throwing them into a sudden convulsion of confusion and alarm. Within five seconds the startled Japanese were wheeling to the right. Within ten they were climbing away, their bombs still undelivered. Then, as they showed their tails, Neal loosed another round. It missed by a wide margin, but accelerated their retreat.

The gun crew, its morale restored, raised a yell of derision and triumph. And the outline of the bombers dwindled until they were merely specks quickly vanishing in the dazzling heat-laden wastes of the eastern sky.

Wilkinson, with *Li Wo* under way, decided that the original escape plan – to hide by day and steam by night – was no longer practicable. The aircraft returning to base would call up a swarm of eager searchers. The ships must split up, stake everything on an all-out dash.

Cook flashed back his approval of Wilkinson's intention. A signal which was to be their last farewell.

Banka Island was just eighty miles away ...

The air attack, or rather the defection of the stokers, had knocked hell out of Murray: Stanton was shocked by his appearance. Jimmy could have borne the Jap aggression with dour defiance; but he was not a particularly strong man physically, and had recently been doing the work of six. He was lying back in his chair ... white faced, shaken, and so played out that he wouldn't even accept a drink until he'd told his story.

The panicking stokers had left him to run the engines almost single-handed. Hearing only the crack of the guns, the shattering explosions of the bombs, he had been working between two boilers and firing six fires. Even the trimmers had run away and hidden behind the sacks of coal on T-deck.

'I'd like to shoot the bastards,' Murray said angrily.

Stanton, with memories of the heat and noise prevailing in the stokehold even in normal times, was amazed by the spirit that had kept his friend working; but all the same he was concerned for the future. Murray could not be expected to do it again. Yet the ship depended so much on his stamina and skill.

He handed Jimmy a stiff whisky; then went to see the CO.

'It's a rum old do,' said Wilkinson. 'I've never known anything like it.'

Through twenty-six years of sea experience, which included a spell in an auxiliary cruiser during the First World War, Tom Wilkinson had encountered many unorthodox situations. He'd ridden storms of argument as bouncily as a buoy. But never, until now, had he been confronted by a chief officer requesting permission to keep station in the stokehold. And requesting it for the oddest of reasons – that he feared the black gang would bunk.

A rum old do, indeed, and Wilkie's first reactions were violent. Left to himself he'd have driven the deserters to work at pistol-point. Or maybe a rope's end might serve to do the trick? All the same, he agreed upon reflection, such action might defeat its purpose. Men driven to duty only by fear might well desert again when a greater danger arose. It was essential that the support given to Jimmy should be reliable and willing. The *Showboat*'s speed depended on her steam pressure, and her ability to dodge the bombs depended, very largely, on her speed. It was as simple as that, said Wilkinson. And he could not imagine why the hell the fools aboard couldn't see it that way. Neither could Stanton.

'They'll be put on a charge, sir?'

'They'll have the full treatment. If I'm alive to give it to them,' Wilkinson growled.

In later years Ronald Stanton was to learn to make allowances; allowances for the new intake's lack of experience, their ill-acquaintance with the ship; the fact that they'd endured the death agonies of real warships before being drafted, still dazed by their ordeal, to this naked little river steamer. Yes, Stanton was to learn his tolerance the hard way – but he had not learned it yet.

In fact, as he changed into rig suitable for the stokehold – a woollen singlet, old pants, sweat rag and leather gauntlets – he found himself almost regretting his original offer to help. Dammit, there were plenty of other bods available. Why shouldn't the bloody cowards be beaten back to work again? And why the hell was he volunteering?

It was an hour after tiffin. Wilkinson and Neal were on the bridge. Murray and Stanton were relaxed and taking it easy, discussing whether or not there would be another raid before nightfall. And then, just as they were kidding themselves the *Li Wo* might be fortunate ... the alarm went off again.

With exaggerated unconcern, they placed their pipes between their teeth, heaved themselves to their feet, and then, each picking up a shovel, moved in businesslike style towards the furnaces. But this was too much for the firemen now on watch there. They were stung to the raw at the thought that the officers were presuming to take over their job. 'You leave this business to us,' they protested vigorously. 'We're not the type to run away!'

Stanton, to his subsequent regret, didn't think of taking the names of these proudly defiant men. But he gathered they were survivors of one of the battle-wagons, and so had already experienced the full force of Japanese attack. Yet, here they were, hiding their fear, and angry that their new officers, 'temporaries' at that, were afraid that they might desert their posts.

Ronald Stanton was deeply moved by the courage of the new watch. 'Thanks,' he said warmly.

But however willing these amateurs were, it was obvious that they would need all the skilled help they could get. And the only skilled men were two Chinese who had belonged to the stokehold's original complement. But where the hell were they? It was only when he'd searched the after T-deck that he found them sheltering between two spare propellers. They'd been there, too terrified to move, from the moment the ship left Singapore.

The anger aroused by their abjectness almost overwhelmed him: but he knew that only persuasion, not force, would shift them now.

'English firemen,' he gesticulated contemptuously – 'English firemen cannot do the job. You can slice and rake better. The ship won't go fast enough.' And he described the words with mime.

The Chinese looked more worried than before.

'English firemen cannot make enough steam,' Stanton continued. 'I don't want a bomb to hit the ship. I don't want to drown.'

The two Chinese understood.

Jimmy Murray, appreciating the calibre of the new watch, climbed to the grating that ran above their heads, and transferred his attention to the gauge glass and the water level in the boilers: they'd explode if they ran dry for two or three minutes. He warned the men about this. Lack of supervision, he emphasised, could mean curtains for everyone. But before he could fully explain the set-up he found himself on his back. The ship had heeled around so suddenly that he'd skidded across the greasy deck plates, and hit his head on the handrails.

The attack had begun.

The floor of the stokehold seemed to rise under the amateur black gang's feet. The coal in the bunkers slipped sideways with the roar of an avalanche. Momentarily they pictured the scene on the bridge. God, how they yearned for it. Up top there was the chance to see your enemy, a chance to dodge. There was the hope, if all else failed, of jumping into the drink. But here, between the furnaces, they had no eyes with which to see their foe; no ready exit from the ship's prison. Their ears were half deafened by the turmoil of the engines. Their sight was dazzled by the cascading white-hot clinkers.

Again the *Li Wo* veered. They were short of breath. They were unsteady on their legs. And then they were seized by fear, a fear that the boilers would burst, and one which was to grip them again with each new manoeuvre of the ship: fear that a hit would rip the fragile hull apart and that hundreds of tons of water would pour in and scatter them like straws.

At the first shock Stanton was paralysed by terror. He stood rigid, like a man in a trance. And then the spell was broken.

Jimmy said, 'It won't be long now.'

Somebody else said, 'Wait for it.'

And the first lieutenant, recovering from his fright, grinned round at them, encouragingly he hoped, at the precise moment the bomb exploded. It hurled the sea against the hull with the force of a giant hammer. The ship shuddered, heeled, then levelled out again. And no one spoke.

Another bomb … another … and another. Sweat ran from the skins of the men in the stokehold. Their faces were barely visible beneath the white cowls they wore to protect them from the glare. But Murray was certain of one thing – the morning's debacle would not be repeated. These regulars could be relied upon.

'Don't you worry about us,' one of them yelled. 'We won't rat on the ship.' They were working like automatons with faulty mechanism, the routine pace speeded up to a frenzy of desperate action.

Stanton peered down into the bunker scuttle. The trimmer, though terrified, was still at work. To encourage his efforts the lieutenant waved to him, and shouted a rather banal joke. The words were drowned by the noise, but the man smiled back weakly.

The attack was prolonged, and pressed heavily home. They could occasionally hear the roar of the low-level aircraft, and the answering fire of the Lewis guns, muffled by the thin shell of the *Li Wo*. Whenever the ship was level, or looked like staying level for any appreciable time, the two Chinese, bringing up their fifteen-foot slices, threw open the furnace doors. With faces turned away they raked and sliced with the fervour of men who knew that their lives were in the balance.

Now the stokehold was like hell itself. Small wonder, thought Stanton, dazed by the heat and noise, that the scratch crew of yesterday had found things so difficult to bear. Flames shot from the furnaces. The unleashed heat burned up all the moisture in the air. Then, almost as soon as the doors were slammed shut behind them, the bombs began to fall again.

'But morale isn't bad,' said Murray. 'Not at all bad ... considering.'

The British stokers, when they'd finished their firing, took it in turns to come out of the hold and squat on the grating, their reward just a cigarette and a glass of water. Stanton and Murray made a point of joking with them. 'With a ship like the *Li Wo* and an old man like Tom Wilkinson, we'll dodge any brick they care to throw,' they said.

This reassurance the worn-out, half-collapsing crew would usually greet with a polite, sceptical grin. But now one of them said brightly, 'Shame this little coracle ain't got an electric motor.'

No, morale wasn't bad ...

Jap machine-gun bullets punctured the pipe that supplied the steam to the Holman Projector: Manston nipped up from his post in the engine-room to repair the damage with electrician's tape.

Neal, on the gun platform, did his best with the artillery: but received small thanks from the harassed black gang. Each time he let fly they loudly cursed his efforts. It was difficult to distinguish the crack of the four-incher from the explosion of the bomb. It made the plates quiver, and nerves quiver too.

Wilkinson's evasive steering also caused havoc in the engine-room. Each tilt of the ship hurled the men across the deck, bruising them and burning them.

The attack continued until 3.45 p.m.. By the time it was over, the steamer had been so shaken by near-misses that sea water was pouring through the side door abreast of the stokehold entrance.

When the 'All Clear' sounded they could hardly believe their luck.

One of the ratings said, 'I'd rather go through the *Repulse* bombing ten times over than endure another attack in this old tub!'

And he meant it.

Despite the length and ferocity of the raid, the *Li Wo* had again succeeded in living up to her incredible reputation. Her superstructure was now a total wreck. Doors, bulkheads and ports had been reduced to matchwood. But her engines were still sound, her hull was still sound, and there were no casualties. Best of all, said Wilkinson, she was nearing the end of her obstacle race. In four hours it would be dark, and she would be slipping into the comparative safety of the Java Sea.

Stanton was relatively cheerful when he went up to the chartroom. Ironically, he had developed a confidence in the *Showboat* that even his knowledge of the probable perils ahead could not dispel. The ship had weathered so many Jap-made storms that he had begun to feel, despite his better judgment, an almost superstitious regard for her. Maybe, he thought, she's just destined to be lucky. He began to measure up the distance to Batavia and calculate the arrival time. Allowing the ship a maximum speed of twelve knots – they wouldn't be able to get much more out of her now – she would, he estimated, dock at 7 p.m. next day. He passed the good news to the QM, who had been watching his pre-occupation with hopeful curiosity.

'I'm very glad to hear it, sir ...'

The civil understatement sounded a bit ridiculous, and gave rise to laughter all round. The hands cheered up, and it was good to see their grins again. Only when Stanton went to his cabin to smarten up before returning to the bridge did he remember that the ship was still in great danger.

On top of the debris lay his girl's picture. Despite the protective pillow it had been swept to the deck and was lying face downwards, pock-marked by splintered glass.

Although not usually superstitious, Stanton regarded this as some kind of bad sign for the future.

They went to action stations just ten minutes later. But this time they had more to fear than even the onslaught of the bombers.

Ten ships had appeared on the Li Wo's beam. They were about six miles away, and were unmistakably Japanese.

CHAPTER FIVE

Stand By To Die

'We've had it,' Wilkinson said calmly.

'I'm sorry, sir?'

'I said, we've had it!'

Stanton, considerably shaken, looked again at the convoy.

The ships appeared to have no naval escort. They were proceeding on a course different to that of the *Li Wo*, and seemed intent on their own task.

Puzzled by the CO's statement, he exclaimed, 'We've weathered worse than this before.'

But Wilkinson shook his head.

The preliminaries of the attack on South Sumatra had begun several days before, when a Japanese invasion fleet sailed from Indo-China.

Assembly area and objective were over a thousand miles apart and the convoys were spotted from the air when their voyage was half complete: but the Allies could do little to interrupt them.

Over a sea area that extended from just south of Singapore to slightly north of Australia, the Dutch Admiral Doorman could dispose of only six cruisers and less than a dozen destroyers.

By the time he had succeeded in concentrating the bulk of this mixed force – British, Dutch, Australian and American – the fast-moving Japanese were off the shores of Banka Island.

Which was where the *Li Wo* met them.

Ten minutes passed. It was five past four. The ship had gone off course a little, and Stanton was getting cross-bearings to fix a new course for the Banka Strait. There was a slight haze over the horizon: and the Japanese convoy was dwindling to vanishing point.

Then came the lookout's hail: 'Ship on the starboard bow.'

Stanton, startled, came out of the chart room, fumbling with his glasses.

Wilkinson's voice stayed unusually quiet. 'Ronnie, take a dekko if you please ...'

It was a larger convoy than before: much larger. And the ships were larger, too.

At first, up on the bridge, they tried to kid themselves. 'Could be a British or Dutch force reinforcing Sumatra.' But they knew that it wasn't.

Then Wilkinson, who had been listening to their talk with a sort of paternal indulgence, cut in with, 'All right, lads, let's forget the theories. Ronnie, start to employ that telescope of yours.'

Stanton's telescope – an army officer in Singapore had given it to him rather than save it for the Japs – had a far longer range than the standard issue Service binoculars.

He sent for it now, as ordered, and took a careful look ...

High, sharp-edged prows ploughed through the sultry, sluggish sea. White hieroglyphics splashed vertically from the top of the tall black hulls to the point where the bow-wave peeled backwards from the stem. Long-barrelled guns were perched on every poop, and over each stem flew the sun flag of Japan.

The ships, in line ahead, reached from two points on the starboard bow to four points on the starboard quarter. But two particular vessels, whose position was slightly removed from this neat procession, caught the first lieutenant's attention.

For the nearest of the pair was a fleet destroyer. And, hull down on the horizon, was a Japanese cruiser.

'Now all that is left to do,' said Wilkinson, 'is for us to go down fighting.'

Silence fell over the bridge: the silence of men who wondered if their ears had played tricks on them. But the CO's next words assured them that they hadn't.

'We'll have a crack at those yellow bastards,' he said. 'I'm going to take one with me!'

Stanton felt as though splinters of ice had penetrated his spine. Wilkinson's attitude was quite incredible. Surely he couldn't mean it?

'But why not try to get away?' he urged. 'We're small; well camouflaged … could take advantage of the mist.'

The skipper made no answer.

'Or maybe we could slip down the Gaspard Strait, the other side of the island?'

'Forget it.'

'But sir …'

For a moment the heat, the tension, and his fierce desire for battle got the better of Wilkinson, moving him to insult. 'All right. I'll tell you the truth. Chance of escape or not, I'm going to do something the real Navy has a word for – I'm going to close the enemy. As long as we can inflict damage on the Jap,' he continued grimly, 'it doesn't matter a damn what happens to you, or me, or this bloody steamer either!' 'But it's hopeless, sir. We'd never touch them.' Wilkinson scowled. 'Are you scared. Lieutenant Stanton?'

A shocked silence.

Stanton, his lips tight with anger, answered coldly, 'I'd have thought you would know more about me by now.'

Wilkinson quietened down, rubbed his hand heavily against his close-cropped head, then slapped his palm down vigorously on the nape of his brick-red neck. 'In view of the special circumstances, I'm going to call for volunteers to man the guns.'

'All right,' answered Stanton. 'You can count me as one of them.'

At first, with the little *Li Wo* at maximum revs bearing down upon her enemies, and the Japanese armada constantly looming larger, the captain and the first lieutenant addressed each other formally, as professional acquaintances rather than men who had endured together the seesaw fortune of the flight from Singapore and were now about to take on odds unparalleled since Grenville's Revenge.

Each of them was very human, and therefore fallible. And the cross-exchange, however infantile, had set up a barrier between them that neither knew how to break. And then Doc arrived, with the tea-jug.

'I may be scared,' said the SBA, with a sort of sombre pride, 'but I'm never too scared to win a cup of tea.'

Laughter, near to tears, united them.

The *Li Wo* and the convoy were on converging courses, and the steamer was gradually approaching the head of the enemy column. So far, the Japanese did not appear to have spotted her; or else they were too intent upon reaching their objective to worry about such an insignificant opponent.

But now, with only five miles to go, the destroyer slowly started to turn away from the convoy and point her nose inquisitively in the direction of the *Li Wo*.

On the bridge there were no heroics. Not even a rousing 'D'ya hear' to stir the crew.

'This is it!' said Wilkinson. 'Let's get cracking.'

Murray went to the stokehold, John Manston to the engine room. Stanton joined Derbridge on the gun platform, but paused to visit his cabin on the way and take a last look at his girl's picture.

More prosaically, he also ditched his regulation tin hat. He'd worn it during the air raids, but didn't think its protection would make much difference now.

He felt certain that he would soon be dead.

'But fancy me fading out before I'm thirty-three,' he thought.

He was six weeks short of his birthday.

Down in the stokehold the scarlet and yellow flames of the furnaces tossed chaotic patterns on the white and grey bulkheads, the glittering brass. Shovels clanged into the shifting coal, while the sweat poured freely down Murray's thighs; his hands were blistered.

As the destroyer turned, the *Li Wo* also altered course, moving towards the Japanese line at a much sharper angle than before in order to shorten the distance and to reach her foes sooner. Murray, although grimly aware of the ship's ultimate objective, did not know the reason for this new move and could only guess at it, anticipating at any moment the outbreak of the storm, and meanwhile he divided his attention between the shovels and the steam gauge, the firemen and the voice pipe. He didn't speak at all.

The gauge climbed to the two hundred mark, the highest it had registered since the ship left Singapore.

Stanton on the gun watched the Japanese movements and prepared for the coming battle. He was surprised to find himself resigned to the business in hand. Yet, fatalistic though his attitude was, he was not conscious of any feeling of heroism. He found that he had only one aim in mind – the destruction of the enemy. This was the end for Stanton, so before Stanton departed he must do the maximum damage he could. Not a very Christian outlook for a man about to die. And he wondered what Neal, that staunch Christian, was feeling.

Curiously he asked the New Zealander, 'How are you doing?'

'Butterflies in the stomach – but I wouldn't miss it for worlds!'

Stanton considered the flushed and eager young face. 'No, I'm sure you wouldn't.' Quite obviously this was no time for Christianity.

John Manston, in the engine room, reached for another glass of water. This was a hell of a setting for a man's last drink, and yet, he reflected, the stuff still tasted good.

A slight swell had arisen, affecting the movement of the ship. The *Li Wo* was riding a little heavier, but the range was closing rapidly. Wilkinson glanced at the foam jerking tumultuously around the bows, then glowered at the enemy ahead, his mind absorbed in considering the best way to close in on it.

In all there were fifteen Japanese ships, and Wilkinson's main worry was to get a crack at them without their firing first. The *Li Wo* had only thirty-one four-inch shells left – the rest had been used during the air attack – and it was essential, if Neal was to inflict damage, to get as close as possible to the enemy.

On the other hand, it needed only one single unit of the opposing line to take alarm and the little *Li Wo* would be blasted out of the water before she'd been able to fire a shot. It was a hard test of nerves, this deliberate approach. And yet he was convinced it was the right one.

The distance was decreasing at the rate of half a mile a minute. The destroyer, mercifully, seemed to be taking her time about investigating the small intruder.

Wilkinson studied the cruiser. She was still well to the rear, though her hull was now showing and her eight-inch bricks would soon bridge the distance. The transports were still in line with their guns trained fore and aft, and showed no sign of anticipating his hostile purpose.

The stage was set.

'Best get it over with,' said Wilkinson.

Then he chose his prey – and drove straight at her.

The khaki-clad infantry sprawled over the transport's decks. Every available inch of space had been put to use, and even these former peasants found accommodation cramped.

The small group of bespectacled officers, some with old-style pith helmets on their heads and others with long swords incongruously clanking at their heels, were standing near the forward gun, eager to sight the beaches from which they would march triumphantly to the city of Palembang. It had been rather a dull voyage and they were only mildly interested in the funny little steamer now chugging so determinedly towards them.

Most of those who watched her steady approach assumed she was a straggler from the other column of the convoy: but the navy men, examining her from the bridge, thought differently. She might be a refugee packet, mistaking them for allies: or else, too scared even to run, she was wanting to give herself up.

So the minutes passed, and still there was no alarm. Low-lying in the water, the *Li Wo* looked even smaller than she was, and even the Japs' late awareness that she carried her guns forward instead of aft, as a merchantman should, failed to arouse suspicion. Indeed, the discovery served only to strengthen the view of the majority that the ship was Japanese, part of the invasion fleet. Vigilance relaxed.

In making his hurried plan of attack, Wilkinson had stressed that its only chance of success lay in its extreme improbability. The idea of so small a ship attempting to do them damage would be too fantastic for the Japs to grasp. And, so far, his hunch was working. Only six thousand yards now lay between the *Li Wo* and her quarry.

It was four forty-five. A blob of white shot upwards to the *Li Wo*'s stumpy masthead. Simultaneously another flag shook loose above her stem. Then, just as the two White Ensigns broke in the breeze, an orange flash spread across her nose. Neal's gun had opened fire.

The first shot was short. The second long. But the third pitched squarely on the transport's bridge. Screaming chunks of metal were thrown fiercely through the air, falling on the Japanese soldiers and killing them.

Leading Seaman Thompson and another regular, his pal, were among those on the gun platform with Neal and Stanton. With Thompson laying the gun and his mate training it, they were a disciplined example to the strangely assorted crew.

A deck rating was acting as breech worker; Mac, the Australian, was passing the shells from the racks. And Lieutenant Featherbridge, who had never had anything to do with a four-inch gun before, had become the rammer number.

Neal did the sight setting, Stanton handled the cordite. And high on the top bridge Wilkie towered over them all, dictating to Able Seaman Snow, the helmsman, holding the ship to her course and keeping his eyes trained on the enemy.

No one could tell what strong impulses of tradition, loyalty and obstinacy were working on him as he pursued his decision, this decision that, whatever it might mean to the war effort, must lead inevitably to the death of his ship, and his own death, too. He had sworn he would never be taken.

Stanton had wondered briefly what the CO must be feeling, but now he had ceased to bother. Even his own personal regrets at apparently saying goodbye to whatever life might hold had vanished from his mind. The fight was on.

When they saw their shell hit home the *Li Wo*'s gunners had raised a howl of incredulous joy. But, having hit the enemy once, they were determined to hit him again. And they kept on firing as fast as they could go.

No answering shots came from the transport, which was in considerable confusion. Her decks teemed with khaki. And into this swarm of humanity the British shells tore with terrible execution.

The *Li Wo* was shooting at less than three hundred yards, and the range was decreasing rapidly.

Stanton speedily finished all the cordite in the Clarkson cases; then took it direct from the canisters. Chaos reigned around him, and things were happening so quickly that he didn't even have time to rip the tapes off the bags, let alone carry out normal routine like spotting for the fall of shot.

But this was, in any case, no longer necessary. For the *Li Wo* was steadily closing with her victim, ignoring all the other ships that came crowding up to oppose her. The target was almost impossible to miss.

'Bloody hell,' shouted Ginger. 'It's all against the textbook, but we're not doing too ruddy bad!'

A great roar passed over the masthead, then the sea was churned upwards into a vast exploding mass. The escorting warships had opened fire, and though they were lobbing their bricks from fourteen thousand yards away, their aim was dangerously true.

'I can't hear anything,' bawled Stanton suddenly, as Featherbridge shouted to him. 'I just can't hear a thing …' During practice shots he'd always put cotton-wool in his ears, but this time he hadn't thought about it. Not until now. Not until too late. He felt his ear-drums were breaking. His brain seemed to be hammering against his skull.

A shell from the destroyer hit the *Li Wo*'s superstructure, and the cruiser scored as well. A number of men, with nothing to do, had been ordered to lie in the scuppers. The two shells killed them.

Screams rose from those positioned behind them. And Stanton was dimly aware of the captain calling to Neal to leave the gun and quieten the panic aft. He was also aware of Neal's return. The New Zealander's face was white and strained. He was holstering his revolver.

'Okay, I've fixed it.'

Stanton glanced at the revolver and decided to ask no questions.

Another shell hit the steamer, rocking her from side to side. But they reckoned, rather breathlessly, that the big boys had missed their chance.

The Li Wo's hull was still intact. She was still making maximum knots. And in another minute she would be in the midst of the convoy, where it would be difficult for the warships to get at her without damaging their own side.

The transport had swung sharply away, like a hunted elephant. But Wilkinson was not to be diverted from the chase. The range closed down ... nine hundred yards ... eight hundred yards ... seven hundred yards ... Then someone yelled, 'My God, we've met the armada!'

Several smaller transports – they'd scarcely noticed them before – now seemed to fill the seascape. They were circling wildly round the Li Wo ... were potting at her with their bow guns. These small, vicious weapons threw a three-pound shell, and the smoke and the din almost succeeded in distracting them. But the steep hull of their quarry was now so close to them that it was impossible to miss.

The *Li Wo* hit something – they could all of them feel the bump – and for a moment they thought she had tangled with the wreckage. But as they glanced over the side they saw a mass of struggling bodies of Japanese soldiers who had jumped overboard.

Hundreds of them were around the steamer, screaming in the water as they were caught by her bows or dragged into the mincing machine of the propellers. Hundreds of them … dying horribly … cruelly … cursing their killer.

'The Armada,' Stanton thought crazily. 'Yes, this is how it must have been … ships swanning round at pistol range, smoke hanging over masts and rigging; a bloody great free-for-all …'

There was a burst of fire from one of the smaller ships, gashing a horizontal hole in the *Li Wo*'s starboard side. Shell fragments from the escorting destroyer fell on the boat-deck, a storm of steel. More of the reserve team crumpled dying into the scuppers: but the machine-gunners still fired back from the bridge, killing and wounding the enemy.

Smoke poured from the transport and a ripple of flame raced over her slanting deck. A savage yell came from Thompson as Japanese officers shot at the *Li Wo* with their pistols. The yell was echoed by Wilkinson with four words: 'Stand by to ram!' Stanton, pausing from lifting the cordite out of the canisters, bawled at the CO: 'Don't do it, sir. She's already as good as done for. Don't ram her, sir. Let's have a go at another!'

But Wilkinson did not answer. He was standing in the fore part of the bridge, clinging to a stanchion.

His chin was thrust stubbornly forward, his eyes were fixed on his prey, determined to make sure of her.

When the transport was only a hundred yards away, the *Li Wo*'s gunners ceased to fire, bracing themselves for the inevitable crash. It came ten seconds later.

Travelling at twelve knots and with seven hundred tons of weight behind her, the *Li Wo* plunged her bows into the enemy's port side, ripping it open like a sardine tin. She hit the Jap squarely amidships. The force of the collision had thrown everyone off their feet. For a moment the transport heeled over at an angle of fifteen degrees, and then, shuddering from the impact, the *Li Wo* recoiled and came staggering back ... free of the jagged tangle of broken pipes and plates, victor of the crash that had pushed her bows back to the level of the windlass.

There was a short silence, broken only by the groan of the timbers and the hiss of escaping steam. Then, as the ships began to drift apart, Wilkinson reeled to the voice pipe to give orders to the helmsman. But the steering had broken down. So, too, had the main steam pipeline. And below, although they did not know it, Murray lay dead.

The enemy opened fire again, but this time only the Lewis guns were able to answer back. The four-inch gun was silent.

'All tubes finished, sir.' The breech worker's voice was urgent.

'Blast it!' yelled Neal, frustrated and full of hate at the sight of the targets swanning around the ship. He threw the key of the magazine to one of the ratings. 'For God's sake bring me replacements.' The man moved off, then vanished, swept over the side by the blast from an exploding shell.

Neal said, 'I'm off to my cabin. I've got a spare key there.'

As he ran from the platform, Thompson exclaimed, 'Ain't there anything we can do right?'

Wilding, his mate, pointed at the transport. 'Christ, we've done that job. Done it for keeps!'

No longer needed on the gun, Stanton went up to the wheelhouse. He was anxious to see what he could do to help Snow, the helmsman. But one look at the wreckage convinced him that the steering was beyond repair.

Wilkinson arrived, tried the wheel for himself, swore at its failure to respond, and then, incredibly, gave a broad and happy grin. 'Well, one thing's sure,' he said, with a jerk of his capless head towards the sinking Jap, 'we've got that bastard.'

'Yessir.'

'Which is more than we're ruddy well worth,' said Wilkinson.

Neal returned, eager for action. He had passed the key to Thompson, who was going to collect the tubes. Meanwhile, he was anxious for a job. Any job.

'Good shooting,' Wilkie said, greeting him with quite unusual warmth. 'You've done some damned good shooting!'

But before the New Zealander could reply, an explosion, the loudest so far, reverberated throughout the ship. The planks shuddered beneath their feet. Debris fell on them like hail. Steam roared hysterically through the bisected funnel. Three other near-misses followed in quick succession, nearly deafening them. 'It's the cruiser,' yelled someone. 'She's sending over salvoes!'

It was only when the blast receded and they had picked themselves up from the planks that they became aware of the extensive damage caused by this burst of enemy fire. They realised this with an extraordinary sense of shock. And they looked at the ship as though they were strangers to her, seeing her for the very first time.

They had been preoccupied with the business of attack for so long that their senses had been numbed as to what was happening around them.

The *Li Wo* was in a terrible plight. Her decks were a shambles. The dead lay everywhere.

Wilkinson moved to the far wing of the bridge. He was very quiet, a man drained of all energy and emotion. The *Li Wo*, the ship designed for a peaceful trade, had done incredible things, had performed a feat of arms unmatched for nearly three hundred and fifty years. She had attacked a fleet. She had broken an enemy line. She had destroyed a foe three times larger than herself. Her action had caused the death of hundreds of enemy soldiers. And now it was her turn to be destroyed.

She was surrounded by her enemies, and under fire from all sides. Her ensigns, torn to tatters, were still flying. But her armament was silent. There were many casualties and the survivors could no longer avenge their dead comrades. Wilkinson's attack had served its purpose, but now the *Li Wo* could not be steered, could go no farther. As though awakening from a dream, the captain gave the order, 'Abandon ship!'

The dead lay at the foot of the ladder to the main deck. They were piled on top of one another, directly in Stanton's path. They were terribly mutilated. As the ship's warning system had been destroyed, Neal and Stanton had to pass Wilkinson's order on to those left to hear it: the task was unenviable.

Stanton moved along the empty saloon deck: the *Li Wo* was under continuous fire. Splinters whistled past his ears, but he didn't even duck. He was overwhelmed by the memories of those corpses: his brain pictured nothing else. His head as buzzing, his legs seemed devoid of strength.

He became dimly aware that there were more bodies on the deck below, and that men were swimming beside the ship … men who were not Japanese but members of his crew.

'Abandon ship: Abandon ship!'

The voice, broken and harsh, sounded unlike his own. And then, while he walked the deck and shouted, his mind became obsessed by a tormenting problem.

It was one that was to haunt him in later years, and wake him from his sleep in muck-sweats of guilt, as though he had lost something through his own fault that could never be found again. Something that was more significant to him than anything else.

Who the hell were they, those at the foot of the ladder? 'Oh god,' he wept. 'I don't know. I just don't know … I can't even guess.'

It seemed a terrible thing, this inability of his to identify former comrades. But worse, he did not dare go back and take a second look at them.

'Ronnie.'

The voice sounded as though it came from miles away. 'Ronnie, have you found anyone?'

He looked at Neal with half-incredulous delight, Neal who was as pale and shaken as himself.

'No, only the dead.'

But, by God, it was good to look upon somebody who was still alive: he felt better. He found himself explaining, in a surprisingly normal tone, 'Some of the chaps stopped a packet at the foot of the bridge ladder. But, otherwise, I haven't seen anyone – have you?'

Neal, too, had been unsuccessful in his search.

'Quite a lot killed,' he said. 'But some of the chaps must have jumped earlier. The sea is full of them.'

The thought that others had got off the ship gave them new life. They ran to the shattered wardroom and dragged the table out of the debris to the side of the ship. They thought it would give them something to float on when they, too, took their chance with the water. But in this, as in almost everything else, frustration dogged them. Although with much effort they managed to ditch the table, their plan failed: they hadn't realised that the ship still had enough way to carry the raft astern. It was soon out of their reach.

They started back to the wheelhouse in a state of panic. The search and the tussle with the table had taken only a few minutes, yet it seemed as though they'd been away for hours. They went at the double, heads down. Their renewed instinct for self-preservation made them aware of the fury of the Jap fire. The sooner they got the word to go from Wilkinson, the better.

A man came running out of the cross-alley. He almost collided with them. Then, without warning, he tipped back on his heels, tottered forward and plunged to the deck.

'Dead,' said Neal. 'Out like a light!'

'The lucky bastard. At least it was quick,' muttered Stanton. 'Maybe a shell splinter …'

But the man was not dead. 'For God's sake, don't leave me,' he cried.

'Take it easy,' Stanton said. 'We won't forget to come back.'

The man's cries were still ringing in their ears when they came upon Wilkinson. He hadn't moved since they last saw him. He was leaning on the bridge rail, calm and relaxed.

Neal was to say to Stanton afterwards, 'I'd have given a million to know what the old man was thinking.' But at the time the New Zealander merely reported that with the exception of Jack, the wounded man, the crew were either dead or away.

'Then off you go,' said Wilkinson.

'But what about you, sir?' Neal asked.

With a trace of his sarcastic smile, he said, 'I told you once before. Remember? If I didn't get killed in action I said I'd go down with the blasted ship ...'

'But that's bloody nonsense!'

'It's tradition – didn't you know?'

They did know. They had discussed its merits once or twice in the wardroom for want of something to talk about. But now it seemed a terrible thing to them; a deliberate self-sacrifice, and they stood there aghast and begged him to change his mind.

Wilkinson was impatient and becoming angry, as though afraid that they'd succeed in stealing what little remained to him – his personal integrity, his pledge to himself.

'For the last time, no,' he said. 'And now get out. Get out, the pair of you. Get out while you can.'

They turned away, speechless and sad. But as they were groping their way across the sloping bridge towards the torn main deck, Wilkinson came after them, stopped them, and shook hands with each of them.

'Good lads,' he said. 'You've been good lads. Now beat it ... there's nothing else to stay for.'

A salvo came over to speed them on their way.

CHAPTER SIX

The Death of Thomas Wilkinson

Derbridge and Stanton, dazed by the blast of the salvoes which hurled up volcanoes of foam around the sinking ship, were staggering towards a suitable jumping-off point when they remembered Jack.

The wounded man was still lying in the cross-alley. They must go back. No help for it.

Jack looked up, his face twisted with pain. 'Thanks,' he muttered, then relapsed again into delirium.

They humped him between them to the end of the deck; and hesitated indecisively.

The man was wounded in the stomach and had become unconscious through the acrid fumes of the explosives.

So, how to move him, without killing him?

Stanton climbed down on to one of the depth-charge throwers, and Neal heaved the body into his arms.

Next, Stanton Slid down the ship's side to the rubbing strake, and once again Jack was lowered into his grasp. From the strake it was only a short drop into the water.

'Okay?' he queried, as Neal joined him.

'Okay.'

'Then don't waste time. Let's go.'

Stanton, with Jack in tow, had progressed only a few yards when he realised that Neal was no longer with him. He turned, to see the New Zealander climbing back on to the ship. Well, what the hell? He trod water and shouted. Derbridge shouted back, but his explanation was drowned by the scream of a shell.

'You all right?' The words were almost bellowed in his ear. Leading Seaman Wilding had jumped into the water before them with the Malay W/T operator, a fellow who had stuck to his duty even when the wireless cabin had collapsed about him.

'Can't understand about Mr Derbridge,' Stanton said. 'He's returned to the ship'

They rested, and looked back. Neal was no longer to be seen. Instead, to their surprise, two figures appeared on the fo'c'sle deck. Ginger Thompson and another rating.

'But Neal and I checked to see if there were any survivors. So how the devil did we miss them?' It took Stanton a few agitated moments to get the answer. And then he realised guiltily that they'd been sent below to get those spare tubes for the gun.

The two men looked pathetically small, tragically defenceless against the background of steam, smoke and flames which now framed the *Li Wo*. Yet they showed no sign of leaving. Instead, they just stood there as if waiting for orders, until

Wilkinson himself appeared and was seen to order them over the side.

Thompson's mate was swimming strongly when the next Jap salvo fell.

One of the shells exploded on top of him.

A mighty surge of water swept over the rest of the survivors, filling their ears and mouths and tossing their life-jacketed bodies like corks on its reeling crest. Stanton maintained his hold on Jack, but only with an effort.

And the latter, regaining consciousness, began to yell out.

Tom Wilkinson, now the only man alive in the shell-splintered sinking ship, staggered through the smoke to the near side of the bridge. The swimmers shouted at him to jump: but he took no notice.

He stared at the blazing Japanese transport, hypnotised by the sight of the havoc he had caused, and then looked down on the wreckage-strewn sea.

'They'll never take me alive.' Wilkinson's words echoed in Stanton's mind. He tried to shout, but seawater choked his cries. And then he saw Tom Wilkinson wave and move off towards his cabin.

Stanton yelled, 'For Christ's sake, jump!'

It was stupid, a waste of effort. He knew that even if by some miracle his words could have reached the ship, Wilkie would take no notice. Yet he found himself trying again.

It was Wilding who interrupted him. The Japanese cruiser, after a brief lull, had reopened fire, and the rating had been quick to see the significance of this action. 'They're not aiming at the ship,' he cried. 'They're trying to get us!'

Almost immediately shells began to tear into the water around the swimmers. Stanton's leg numbed to the vicious stab of steel. A shell splinter had lodged in his calf.

Long minutes passed: he was dazed and sick. He was still holding on to Jack, without knowing why. Over the top of a wave he glimpsed what he thought was a life-raft, with men on her. 'Over here! Help!' he shouted. 'I'm towing a wounded man.' But his hail was unanswered and the raft dropped out of sight. The swell was steepening rapidly. So much so that he could now no longer see the swimmers who had been near him. He glanced desperately back to the *Li Wo*, in an attempt to fix his direction. And by doing so was in time to witness the sinking of the *Showboat*.

She was slipping gently, going down bows first.

Then the raft came back.

The raft was all that was left of the ship's one lifeboat. The Japanese, infuriated by their losses, had hurled hand-grenades into her. They had killed most of the original occupants. They had blown open all but two of the buoyancy tanks. Yet she still continued to float. A blood-spattered, broken shell ... yet she still continued to float. More of the men of the *Li Wo* swam over to her. And among them was John Manston.

'No hawkers, no circulars,' was his greeting to Ronald Stanton. He retained enough of his debonair pose to make a joke. But otherwise the dandy 'third' was preoccupied with very serious business.

The Japanese shelling had splintered the shin of one of the survivors, and John Manston, with the help of the sick-bay attendant, was acting as surgeon.

Stanton, grabbing a welcome line, shouted to him: 'I've got Jack here. Can you look after him?'

Manston neatly extracted a fragment of bone and threw it into the sea. 'Glad to try, Ronnie, but the boat's very tender. One more body aboard and she'll turn right over.'

Stanton glanced at the other men. 'Won't one of you give him a place?'

It was a lot to demand of the shell-shocked, distraught survivors. They had won their precarious perch the hard way and were reluctant to abandon it.

'For God's sake,' pleaded Stanton. 'This chap's in agony.'

Gingerly, reluctantly, an AB slipped over the side.

'Thanks,' mumbled the first lieutenant, as Jack was hoisted aboard.

The cruiser ceased fire. There was silence except for Jack's delirious shouting and the distant, despairing cries of men they could not see.

And then, his heart sinking, Stanton heard the quick staccato pulsing in the west.

'Dear God,' he prayed. 'Please let me be mistaken.'

He was still praying when the Jap ship that was annihilating the survivors hove into view.

She was small, about five hundred tons. Originally she had been left behind to pick up the survivors of the transport, but now she was seeking vengeance on her enemies. Having spotted the lifeboat, she steered directly for it. She was steaming very slowly, at two or three knots, they thought.

And she hit the boat amidship, rolling her right over.

'Swine ... filthy ...' an AB screamed.

They were the last words he ever uttered. His body jerked backwards ... then folded like a jack-knife. He sagged, face downwards, in the water ... riddled with bullets.

Stanton, striking out vigorously to clear the enemy's propeller, came alongside two men in khaki, manning a Vickers machine-gun. For a horrific second he found himself looking straight up into its barrel. And, in that second, the Japanese let fly.

Every nerve cried out in agony. Momentarily he blacked-out. A bullet had passed through the back of his head.

When he came round he found himself about ten yards from the Jap ship. He put up his hands to his head, to feel the damage: and the first three fingers went inside the wound.

With a curious detachment he watched the soldiers traverse the gun at his comrades, then swing it back; to draw another line on him. He was aware of someone shouting: 'Swim away!' But he made no movement. He was past caring what else they might do to him. He felt he'd seen everything.

Once more came the quick staccato. Only this time, apparently, he was suffering no hurt. Moisture spilled on to his face. Briefly he'd the illusion that it was raining. But the rain turned out to be sea-water ... driven by bouncing bullets hitting the water around him.

He thought, with irritation, why don't they get it over with? Then noticed that the Japanese were in trouble with the Vickers. He wondered objectively what had gone wrong. But now they were feeding the gun by hand, and maybe the belt had jammed.

There was one further burst of fire before the angle of the ship, passing diagonally ahead of him, shut of the gunners from view. It was a very short burst, far off the target, but Stanton's ordeal was by no means over.

All hands appeared to have mustered on the afterdeck, with the intention of making his send-off really memorable. As he drifted helplessly towards the stern they pelted him with firewood ... heavy faggots used for fuel.

One of the logs came straight towards his wounded head. He raised his arm automatically to defend himself, and the impact split his hand wide open. Blood poured from his fingers.

And then the transport was chugging away from him: its crew searching out other victims.

Why hadn't they managed to kill him? Dear God, why hadn't they? A bullet would have been more merciful than this agonising lingering on the empty sea.

Stanton was still cursing providence when a long white piece of timber rolled into sight. It disappeared ... then reappeared again ... repeated the trick, and seemed to be coming closer. But it wasn't until its hide-and-seek performance had been repeated several times that Stanton, in a dazed condition, was able to identify it. And as he did so, desire for life returned.

The lifeboat, upside down but still afloat. He swam towards it.

But only when he rested his cheek against its rolling hull did he realise what the choppy sea had hidden from him – he was no longer alone.

From all directions men were converging on the boat, including most of those who had been involved in the capsizing. Even the wounded were coming alongside, Jack being towed by a burly AB. And then he came face to face with Ginger Thompson. And Thompson was followed, incredibly, by Neal.

'What the hell happened to you?' he asked the New Zealander blankly. 'I thought you'd gone back aboard ...'

He understood him to answer, 'Went to my cabin to pray ...'

To pray? Went back to his cabin to pray? Stanton tried to puzzle it out, but found the effort too great.

'The lieutenant jumped just after I did,' Ginger said, 'and we struck towards you, in the hope of joining you. But then we heard the machine-gun, so decided to stay well clear. Thanks to that, and the swell, the bastards didn't see us.'

Now they were reunited they decided to try to get the lifeboat right side up. It was a task to which all but the badly wounded applied themselves with great energy. Some of the men climbed on to the boat's bottom, tugging at the keel, while others shoved upwards from the opposite side of the gunwale. Despite their exhaustion they found the task much easier than they'd imagined. But righting the boat was only part of the battle. The Japs had done severe damage to the lifeboat, as a result of which her behaviour was, to say the least, erratic. Her gunwale rested six inches beneath the surface: as one of the men still had the wit to put it, she was almost a submarine.

Loading her proved to be a depressingly delicate procedure. Stanton had planned to position the survivors so that their weight could be distributed evenly, but this job required much experiment. Even the slightest extra weight on the sides and the battered boat turned over. Ages seemed to pass before he got her trim right. She kept capsizing again and again, and each time they had to heave her back. The men managed to climb in eventually via the stern. Once aboard, they were so carefully balanced that they hardly dared move.

This was the prelude to the most terrifying night any of them had ever experienced.

CHAPTER SEVEN

Ordeal By Water

They were only twenty miles from land, but it might as well have been hundreds for all the difference the distance made to their chances of survival. The oars had been destroyed in the initial Jap attack, but oars would not have been of much help to them now.

The boat, if it could still be called such, was quite unmanageable.

As dusk fell, and the night closed in, the only thing to give the despairing men even the slightest comfort for their pains was the sight of the *Li Wo*'s savaged victim. A mass of flames, burning fiercely in the dark, and topped every now and then by one of the shells she carried soaring like a rocket into the shrouded sky. Considering her lethal cargo, she was taking a long time to die.

Yet even this impressive sight ceased after a while to provide a justification for the *Showboat*'s sacrifice; it became instead the mocking symbol of her survivors' helplessness. For, as the hours dragged by, the constant glow of the burning made it obvious to them that the tide, their only hope, had played the traitor. They were drifting within a few hundred yards of the spot where they'd first embarked.

A sombre silence fell over the chilled men, broken only by the cries of the wounded.

Stanton was perched forward, clutching hold of the lifting-hook. His legs were spread over the gunwale. Each oncoming wave caught him under the belly, lifting him upwards, then dropping him again. He was swallowing salt by the bucketful, and bleeding like a stuck pig. Every time he touched his injured head the blood from his damaged hand flowed downwards, drenching his arm to the elbow.

The W/T operator passed him a handkerchief to cover his scalp wound and hold the loose skin firm. But in seconds the linen was sodden and moulded to his skull. He was convinced that only two alternatives – faced him: either he would bleed to death or else, becoming too weak to hold on, he would drift away and drown.

Jack's plight was the most pitiful of all. He lay amidships, quite helpless, the waters surging through his mouth and nose. And every few minutes, maddened by the agony of his wounds, he would struggle frenziedly with the patient Rogers: obliged to hold him down for fear he upset the boat.

It was nearly dawn before this tortured man found release from his pain in death.

Morning came: and brief delusive hope. Adrift on the glittering swell they saw what they thought was a pair of koleh rafts. Stanton slipped over the side, in an effort to swim to them, but they were not visible from water level. He stayed only a few minutes in the rapidly steepening swell: then realised that he'd lost sight of the boat. He was in a state of panic until Manston's voice guided him back.

He wondered afterwards why he was still clinging to life when this merely prolonged his agony.

The next move of the survivors in their attempt to gain the rafts was to be equally abortive. Ripping some broken sideboards from the boat, they tried to use them as paddles. For a time they were able to kid themselves they were slowly closing the distance. They were almost convinced of success when the boat turned over again. By the time they'd succeeded in laboriously righting her, the kolehs had drifted out of sight.

At noon a Jap aircraft came over, flying low. Half hopefully, half fearfully, they followed her flight, wondering whether she would mean massacre or rescue.

But the plane merely circled them. Then flew away.

Two Japanese destroyers hove into sight a little later. Once more the *Li Wo* survivors roused themselves from their stupefying apathy. Stanton said, with more assurance than he felt, 'The naval types are different from other Japs. They've got quite a chivalrous code.' But the chivalrous warships also turned away.

The fate of those who'd served in the bellicose little *Showboat* how seemed abundantly clear.

Slow death, with thirst and madness, and a grave far down at the bottom of the sea.

Neal said, evading Stanton's gaze, 'I'm going for a swim.'

Thompson said, 'Okay, sir. I'll go with you.' Stanton protested, 'Don't be so bloody daft ... But they were away before he could think up a more convincing reason to hold them back.

An hour went by: the swimmers had failed to return. Another hour, and he found himself actually envious of their fate. He'd called them bloody daft. But they didn't seem so crazy now. Through lips crusted with salt, he croaked to Manston, 'John, let's follow their lead. A long swim ... and a quiet dive to the bottom.' The 'daft' suggestion now seemed to him the only sensible plan ... a short cut to paradise.

But his comrade had not yet experienced the fevered effects of the salt thirst. 'Steady, Ronnie,' he warned. 'You don't know what you're saying.'

'But it's better than staying here ... let's choose our own time to die.'

The reply was unexpected. 'Ronnie, you can't. You happen to be in command.'

'In command? Me? In command of this wreck?'

'In command of men – what's left of them!'

Stanton grasped the lifting-hook tighter. Sledgehammers still beat against his wounded head. Yet Manston was right. And he was still sane enough to see it. He couldn't shirk his duty. Half grudgingly he forced himself to plan ... but plan, this time, with constructive purpose.

The Japanese transport was still afloat. For the past twenty-four hours they'd been aimlessly circling her. She was no longer a ship, but a burned-out hulk. But supposing she happened to be equipped with a steel boat? Or had flesh water in her tanks? She was about four miles away, and he didn't think that any one of them could make the distance to her; but at least they might try …

He told the men what he proposed to do. 'Any of you like to come with me?'

'I'll have a go, sir,' the sick-bay attendant answered, 'though I don't give much for our chances.'

'Nor I,' said Manston. 'I'd say they were almost nil.' Then he added, with an echo of his old casual charm: 'However, I'll string along … at least it will be worth a try.'

It was unbelievably difficult to maintain direction. The sea was so rough that they could see their objective only when it reeled drunkenly to the crest of an extra high wave. The boat they'd just left was soon out of sight.

The SBA was willing in spirit. But the flesh betrayed him. By no means a strong swimmer, he found it impossible to keep up the heavy going. After a while he turned back to look for the boat. Manston and Stanton were left to continue on their own.

Yet, after the next minutes of endless struggle, even Stanton began to regret his decision. 'We haven't a hope in hell of getting anywhere,' he panted, 'so what's the idea?'

'Damned if I know, but we might as well press on. There's no alternative left ...'

The waters pounded their heads and bodies. The kapok life-jackets rubbed against their chins and armpits. They found it increasingly difficult to keep together. The tide's strength, and their own weakness, caused them to drift apart. Three times they lost touch with one another, and three times were reunited. Later they became so widely separated that they could only catch glimpses of each other, and then only when riding the top of a wave in this switchback sea.

Once when he caught sight of him, Stanton noticed that Manston had found a piece of timber, and was using it as a surfboard. Later he saw his friend gesticulate and appear to be shouting, but it was impossible to hear what he was calling.

'Maybe,' Stanton thought wildly, 'he's trying to warn me of sharks. But what the hell? I've thought of them already!'

He was losing enough blood to attract any number of the brutes, but there were no fins in sight. Again he saw Manston, and again the latter waved to him. And then John Manston disappeared for good.

Doggedly, yet despairingly, the first lieutenant continued to swim. He found side-stroke the easiest, and kept direction by using a cloud as a fix. But all the time he was swallowing the salt water. However much he tried to prevent it, the stuff came at him, came at him in full flood. And it was going down his throat ... salt by the bucketful.

He stopped swimming. He put his hands over his face and turned his back on the waves.

Running taps and cool, clear streams ... tall glasses of fresh water ... He could think of nothing else.

The ship seemed almost as far away as when he'd started the journey. He could see no sign of the boat. When darkness fell he would be completely lost. But worst of all was the thought of the salt ... salt by the gallon. He'd be swallowing the stuff until he died: in madness probably. So his mind turned back to the plan he'd formed earlier. Why not shorten his agony?

'You're in command,' Manston had said. But damn that. He'd nothing left to command. Not now. No one looked to him for leadership, no one depended on him. He was all alone in the hostile wilderness of the ocean.

He took off his life-jacket and dived. He swam downwards as far as he could go. He drew in great gulps of water and salt. His stomach expanded with pain so excruciating that he blacked-out. And yet, when his brain cleared, he found he was back on the surface.

This awakening came as a malicious anti-climax. Angered, he determined to try again. This time he must find release. And yet once more the fickle sea rejected him.

In all, Ronald Stanton made five attempts at suicide. After the fifth his stomach was so distended and he was in such pain that he could not stop himself from screaming.

He struggled to find his life-jacket and then to get back into it. The effort and the pain caused yet another black-out.

He was in the Singapore club, shouting at a boy to bring him water … tall glasses of iced water, after the daily swim. But the boy only leered and took no notice of the order. Obviously, he must go himself, if he really wanted service. But however much he tried, he couldn't stand up. And now his body had turned to solid salt. The planters, monopolising the next table, didn't listen to his cries. 'Water!' he mumbled. 'Water! For pity's sake get me water!'

He came to. He was trying to belch and couldn't … was trying to get rid of the salt that blistered his mouth and belly. But he couldn't belch. He could only groan and choke. Another wave hit him and then another: but he hardly noticed them. The salt was by now nearly solid in his throat … the salt that stung his eyes, clogged his ears and rolled from his smarting nose.

A glittering social event aboard the flagship … punkah fans whirring above a chattering crowd … cool breezes blowing from a gaily lit shore. And the drinks were arriving, on a shining silver tray. Water … lovely water … glass after glass of it.

He was screaming when he regained consciousness. The movement and gathering violence of the sea terrified him. He was hopelessly alone, a solitary human lost in a vast primeval world.

'Water,' he sobbed. 'Clean water …'

And at last he was able to belch.

Stanton must have thrown up several gallons of sea-water before he began to recover his senses. Five attempts to die had failed. Best, after all, to leave his death to chance.

'I will go on swimming,' he decided. 'Any direction will do. I will swim until I peg out.'

But he was still alive and afloat when darkness began to fall.

He came suddenly upon a broad patch of discoloured water, a deep brown valley, in the half-light, between silver-green peaks. Somehow he became obsessed with the idea that this would be less salt than the rest of the heaving waters. He buried his face into the muddy patch and drank deliberately.

It was brackish and tepid stuff, and only when the salt-sickness again tore into his still-swollen belly did he stop his frenzied swallowing.

And then, with pain jerking him almost upright in his life-jacket, he saw the raft ...

It was only a few yards away. But he refused to get excited: he'd been deceived before. The club ... the iced drinks ... all part of his delirium. He closed his eyes.

But when he looked again the raft was still there, tossing on the swell. There were men aboard it.

'Please come to me,' he screamed, in a voice he hardly knew.

The voice that answered him, he knew extraordinarily well. It came from Neal Derbridge – whom he'd given up for dead.

Neal and Thompson had been at the end of their tether when they'd found the raft in the early afternoon.

It was occupied by an Australian stoker, a man called Maury. He told them he'd climbed aboard it just after the *Li Wo*'s sinking: and had been on his own ever since.

Composed of airtight metal compartments in a wooden frame, the raft measured only four and a half feet by four. The shortage of space caused by Stanton's arrival was acute. By discarding their life-jackets the men were just able to make sufficient room for three of them to lie down at a time. The fourth had to sit precariously on the edge.

They decided to take turns in occupying these positions, the most favoured being that of the man in the centre, who got some comfort from the bodies around him. For most of the time, however, even he was freezing cold. With so much weight aboard it, the raft had sunk to within three inches of the surface. About one wave in every four swept over it. Though desperately tired, the men were only able to sleep fitfully.

At one stage Stanton woke up to find Neal delirious ... babbling about the beloved destroyer in which he'd served before joining the *Li Wo*.

He kept pointing into the darkness, insisting that he could see her ... that the ship was coming alongside ... that at any moment they'd be scrambling up her sides.

Stanton, though still half-crazed by thirst – the raft had no water – kept enough sense to see the danger in Neal's condition. Should Neal fall over the side, they'd be too numb and weak to rescue him.

Yet as soon as Stanton persuaded him to lie down, the New Zealander's mind again began to wander.

'We're hitting them, lads,' he cried. 'We're hitting them. Come on. Let's hit them again!'

In his delirium he was reliving the battle with the convoy.

'Land!' Neal shouted. 'God, man ... I tell you, it's land!'

Stanton woke up. Neal had shaken him by the shoulder. The action cured the numbness which had anaesthetised his hand. Fresh stabs of pain shot through his arm. Blast Neal, and these damned mirages. And blast the ties of comradeship and memory that bound one to him ...

'Land,' the New Zealander was repeating wildly. 'Look! ... over there! ... it's the land!'

Stanton eyed the scene with a bleary eye. The first streak of dawn had appeared, but it was still ice-cold. Hatingly he glared at the waters around the raft ... hatingly at the blood clotting on his arm. And then, as he struggled to his elbow, he saw the cause of Derbridge's excitement.

Banka Island lay only five miles away.

'See what I mean!' the New Zealander exclaimed.

'This means water,' mumbled Stanton, 'lots and lots of lovely water.'

He could think of nothing else.

Thompson and Maury awoke. As unbelievingly as Stanton they gazed at the black line of the shore.

'We've beaten the bastards,' Thompson shouted, 'The *Showboat*'s beaten the bastards!'

They looked at each other, four out of a crew of more than ninety. They wanted to cry.

And then Maury's voice cut through their excitement. 'Okay, so it's land. But tell me how we get there!'

CHAPTER EIGHT

On The Beach

Stanton replied sharply, 'We'll paddle her there, you fool.'

Maury gesticulated exhaustedly. 'Then we'll have to use our hands …'

The pieces of driftwood they'd retrieved for paddles had been swept overboard during the night. They'd just been too tired to notice.

Thompson said, 'But maybe the current will do the job for us. It's running towards the shore.'

Stanton shrugged. 'It's not good enough. May change before we get there.'

'Then what the hell do we do?'

'What Maury says. We'll use our ruddy hands.'

He didn't say anything more. His swollen tongue seemed to block his parched mouth. Each word was formed painfully: required incredible effort.

His three comrades were also silent. Installed in new positions, one at each corner of the raft, they displayed to begin with a sort of fierce despairing energy: but it was impossible to sustain. Even at the best of times the raft, which was almost square, would have been difficult to steer. It was liable to get out of control and turn in circles. But this was the worst of times for the crew of battle-scarred men. And as the hated sun climbed higher in the sky, the men had to fight against a great desire to sleep. The tall trees which Stanton was using as a fix shimmered and danced before his aching eyes. There were intervals when they disappeared completely ... incidents accompanied by a relapse into his former dream-world.

Once he found himself reliving a conversation with Tom Wilkinson: about the fact that no official camouflage scheme had been introduced for the flotilla. 'You got ideas?' the latter snapped at him. 'Then bloody well go act on 'em. I'll carry the can.'

This memory of the time when they'd disguised the *Li Wo* – a process laughed at, but copied later by sister ships – was followed by a nightmare.

Wilkie's voice ended it ... 'Are you scared, Mr. Stanton?' ... And the Number One awoke, finding himself in the water.

Though partly recovered from his delirium. Neal, too, had terrible moments of relapse. Whatever it was he'd done, when quietening the panic-stricken men after the first Japanese hits, seemed to prey on his mind. Repeatedly he felt for his jettisoned revolver. Repeatedly, too, though in happier mood, he reverted to the destroyer. A happy ship, Stanton thought in a moment of coherence, to have such a hold on the New Zealander's affection. But the thought was interrupted by a loud oath. Ginger Thompson's turn, this time, to fall into the drink!

Four enfeebled men ... two of them wounded ... all of them maddened by thirst – years rather than hours seemed to pass in their despairing odyssey.

They were still two miles from the shore when a motor-launch appeared ...

The launch had seemed to come from nowhere. It had rounded a headland, was approaching them at speed. White plumes of spray shot upwards from its nose. Its engine note was rising to a fierce assertive roar.

They watched it with sudden resignation, unsurprised, even without curiosity.

Thompson guessed, 'It's bound to be a Jap.'

Stanton merely nodded. He couldn't have cared less.

Twenty-four hours before, the sight of the intruder would have filled them with hope and terror ... hope of rescue ... terror of Jap massacre. But now they were passive. They felt powerless to influence their fate. The sea had already made such cruel sport with them that human foes seemed of very small account.

The launch came within hailing distance ... circled them once or twice ... carved a wide swathe of foam that almost upset the raft. And then, its engine suddenly stilled, it rode alongside.

Well, this is it, thought Stanton. The moment they kill us ...

He was so dazed by the noise that, like the others, he didn't understand the significance of the words that someone in the launch was shouting at them. It was only after emphatic repetition that they realised what was happening. They were being hailed in English. The 'Jap' was a British ship.

They were so weak that their legs collapsed beneath them when they tried to stand up. They had to be helped inboard.

The launch's CO was wearing RAF uniform. A large white flag was flying at the masthead. For a moment, however, they did not even notice these unusual details: nor even if they had would they have asked for an explanation. They were only concerned with the fact that at long last they would have something to drink: lots and lots of lovely water.

Gently the cox'n assisted them aft, until they were able to lie down in the cockpit. Then, having propped them up like straw dummies, he handed them a tin mug and unscrewed the top of a five-gallon drum. Water! Lots and lots of lovely cool water ... The liquid was highly chlorinated, and by no means cool: but they relished every drop.

Stanton emptied the mug five times; not even griping stomach pains could teach him the need for caution. Someone handed him a packet of Arnott biscuits. He took just one bite, then was forced to spit the stuff out. He couldn't swallow anything but water. Not at this stage. Nor did he really want to. He returned ecstatically to the tin mug.

Minutes passed before he began to take stock of his surroundings. The result astonished him. The launch was crowded with wounded.

'But how come,' he asked himself, 'that I didn't spot them before?'

He was so astonished at the fact, and at his failure to have appreciated it, that for the moment he almost refused to believe it. But it wasn't a dream. Not this time. The wounded were everywhere.

They were lying in the cabin. They were lying on the skylight top. There was even a row of them stretched on the engine casing. One man, he saw with horror, had torn stumps for legs. Others were covered, mercifully, by blankets.

'Burn casualties,' said a voice, 'and all of them bloody awful!'

'My name's Twentyman. You feeling better?' It was the launch's CO speaking.

With an effort Stanton steadied his wandering, shocked gaze. 'Yes, tons better … thanks to you. But what's been happening? And where do we go from here?'

The CO hesitated. 'I'm sorry, old chap. I'm afraid I've some rather bad news. You see,' he added slowly, 'this craft is bound for Mundok.'

'Mundok?' A puzzled pause. 'But I'm afraid I don't understand,' said Stanton. 'We heard that the new Japs were already in Mundok.'

Twentyman nodded. 'Yes, I'm afraid they are.'

He pointed to the masthead, and the limp white flag. 'See that, old chap? We've had to strike our colours. These chaps here are prisoners, and we're en route for the bag!'

Bound for the bag. For the mercies of Japan? They stared at the first lieutenant in disbelief. Here they were on a British ship … saved as they'd thought after all … and the British ship was voluntarily proceeding to Japanese captivity.

Twentyman must be off his bloody rocker.

Stanton said, dazedly, 'But you can't really be serious?'

Twentyman answered grimly, 'Never been more so in all my life.'

He pointed at the wounded. 'And there are the reasons. They've got to have their chance, even though it's pretty slim – the poor bastards. But before you go barmy,' he added, 'better give you the form ...'

Twentyman's story was a strange one. The launch had been in company with a sister ship when a Japanese force attacked. Right from the start the odds had been hopeless. The small craft were opposed by destroyers twenty times their size. They could match only light machine-guns against the enemy's massed artillery. Soon the leading launch was on fire and sinking, and the Japs were turning their attention to Twentyman's command. But then, when her company was waiting for what seemed to be inevitable death, the enemy, astonishingly, had turned magnanimous! They'd spared her to pick up the wounded and proceed 'on parole' to Mundok.

'Extraordinary. Quite extraordinary,' said Stanton when Twentyman finished. 'But why keep to the bargain now?'

The airman answered, 'And I thought you understood!'

To Twentyman, it transpired, the 'parole' had meant very little, a mere expediency. In total war one couldn't afford to choose. But – and here was the rub – there were the casualties to be considered. They needed attention. Needed it desperately.

'Many are very far gone,' he said. 'The burn cases worst of all. And, whatever the Japs may do to us at Mundok, there's one thing clear for sure ...'

'What's that?'

Said Twentyman quietly, 'That these boys will die, the bulk of them, if they don't get there damned quick!'

Stanton said, 'And you? You mean that you'll go, too?'

He shrugged. 'Someone's got to look after them, old chap.'

The pause that followed was broken by Derbridge. 'You are,' he said, 'a much braver man than me.' 'Or me,' added Ronald Stanton. And he meant it.

A handkerchief to tie up Stanton's head ... four tremendous mugs of tea ... their new friend regretted he could not do more for them. But his wounded must come first.

The whole of Banka Island was now in Jap hands. The Jap invasion fleet, minus the *Li Wo*'s victim, was spilling its contents across the shores of Sumatra.

The four men from the *Showboat* could, Twentyman said, if they wished, go with the launch to Mundok. Otherwise he would help them to the beach, should they decide to make an escape bid across Banka, in the slim hope of winning a native boat.

They were still feeling sick and exhausted. Their limbs were covered with salt sores. Yet they surprised themselves by the promptness of their answer.

'Give us the beach,' they said.

It was like an echo of Tom Wilkinson.

The thrill of feeling land beneath their feet was quite extreme. They revelled at the sight of its colour, the lush colour they thought they would never see again. They knew, of course, that the going would be tough. But it was only after they'd waved goodbye to their friends they began to realise how tough.

None of them had shoes, so they were forced to stick to the beaches, where they felt very conspicuous. Hundreds of eyes could be watching them from the safe cover of the jungle. They became depressed, too, by the evidence, everywhere apparent, of the enemy's complete dominance of the waters off the island. One beach they came to was littered with wreckage. On another they found the carcase of a sister ship to the *Li Wo*: shell-torn, partly gutted, and most of her under water.

The strength they'd partly recovered aboard the launch began to ebb again. Their limbs were chafed all over. They walked with bent knees, their legs spread wide apart. 'We look like a bunch of crabs,' was Thompson's comment.

But nevertheless they kept on walking.

It was Stanton's aim to put as many miles as possible between his party and Mundok. He felt that the bulk of the Japanese would be concentrated there. Elsewhere, he argued, their ground forces would be meagre. It wouldn't be worth their while to patrol the whole of the island.

Soon, however, he began to have second thoughts. There were too many traces of Jap army activity. The islanders' homes were deserted, with everything left as if their owners had fled at a moment's notice. They passed a kampong which was completely burnt out. Charred bodies were visible among the cinders.

'Wonder what they did this for?' queried Thompson.

'Keep going,' answered Stanton. 'It's probably nothing compared with what they'd do to us.'

A mile farther on they discovered the first signs of life: half a dozen Malays.

It was obvious from the start that the islanders wished to be friendly. They brought the *Li Wo* survivors coconut milk to drink, and escorted them to a well where they were able to swill down. But it was equally obvious that they were dead scared: they seemed terrified even to mention the Japanese. One man said, unhappily, the soldiers of Nippon were everywhere. His companions immediately shushed him. They kept looking furtively at the jungle fringe behind them, as though expecting immediate interruption. Before leaving they begged the Europeans to hide, and made gestures, sickeningly descriptive, illustrating the fate that might await them if they didn't.

What to do next? The survivors, on their own again, were not quite sure. Lie up for the night? Or try to press on? They were still undecided when they heard a scream of pain. It panicked them all. Conversation came to a stop.

Seconds later Neal Derbridge whispered, 'I think whoever it is is in the bushes ...'

And only after the cry had been repeated several times did they steel themselves to investigate.

'He's one of ours!' exclaimed Maury with astonishment.

It was another *Li Wo* survivor.

A Malay QM, he was lying on his face and convulsed with tremendous pain. Yet, though they examined him they could find no trace of external injury. Nor could they understand how he had reached the shore. To all their questions he replied with groans and cries, and pleaded naively to be sent to hospital. 'As though,' said Thompson, 'there's one just around the corner.' But otherwise? Both his presence and his illness were complete mysteries to them.

The discovery of the QM, however, had one decisive effect. It put an end to their argument and swung the balance, already heavily weighted by their weariness, in favour of finding a temporary resting-place. After forty-three hours in the water and their barefoot trek for miles across the beaches, they felt they had earned at least a short rest. Again they found a convenient hiding-place only a few yards away, a shed in which dry coconuts were stored, an atlap structure with a sandy floor.

Yet as soon as they had settled down, Stanton, for one, regretted the decision. Once out of the sun he was seized by violent shivering. Never, not even on the raft, had he felt so cold before. Security worries also began to torment him. True that the door faced seawards and the shed itself was well screened from the village track: but most of the locals knew of the party's whereabouts. How far was he justified in trusting the Malays?

The delirious cries of the QM lying beside him haunted Ronald Stanton's long periods of wakeful worrying, and penetrated even into his nightmares.

It was nearly dusk. The hut was full of visitors. RAF men.

Stanton, now awake, demanded: 'Where the hell did you spring from?'

Leading Aircraftman Tait answered for them: 'From the same place as you – the sea!'

The newcomers had been through a terrifying ordeal. The launch in which they were trying to escape to Java had been overtaken and sunk. They were only seven strong when they'd first waded ashore. Since then their numbers had been further reduced to five.

'Jap soldiers caught the other two.' explained Tait. 'They bayoneted them in cold blood.'

'Yes,' said his comrade, young LAC Smead. 'They murdered them – just for the fun of it.' Stanton, still astonished, was trying to get the details when one of the *Li Wo* men said, 'The killers were probably the Japs who passed by here ...'

'Japs? Here?'

'Yes, sir, while you were asleep. Six of them!'

'Well,' Stanton said feebly, 'thanks for letting me know.'

Thompson intervened. 'There was no sense in waking you, sir. There was nothing you could have done. They were fifty yards away, so we just lay doggo, and prayed!'

CHAPTER NINE

The Brave Endeavour

Japanese soldiers. Six of them. And within fifty yards of the shed!

Slowly recovering from the shock of realising that his sleep had nearly been eternal, Stanton said, 'Well, if they missed us in daylight they're not likely to come back and find us in the dark.'

'So we might as well stay put?' Tait asked.

'Yes, until dawn. Then we'll shift as fast as we can.'

Thompson looked hopefully at the RAF men's haversacks and kitbags. 'You didn't think to pack the odd revolver?'

'No,' one of them answered, miserably. 'We had to ditch our shooting irons as we struggled for the shore!'

'Then how the hell,' asked Thompson, 'did you manage all this gear?'

'We returned to the launch to get it at low tide.' A depressed silence followed, until Tait added, 'But it's packed with grub, and you're very welcome to share.'

They cheered up at this and settled down to planning the future over a meal of sardines washed down with water.

Stanton was still convinced that the Japanese would be too preoccupied with their Sumatra invasion to have the will, or the resources, to supervise the remoter areas of Banka. Therefore, he aimed to trek across the island from north-west to south-east.

'This side, with Sumatra opposite, they're bound to exercise a pretty stiff control,' he reasoned, 'but they can't be in strength everywhere. So, however hellish the journey overland, I think it's worth a try.'

'And if we make it, sir?' The question came from Smead, a pink-cheeked teenager, youngest of the airmen.

'Ah, if we make it,' said Stanton, 'and if we get a boat … then we'll head down the Gaspar Strait, using the islands for cover until we run for Java.' He paused. 'Well, what do you think of it?'

Unanimously, the RAF men said, 'We'd like to come along, too …'

Stanton was immensely moved by their decision. He had half-expected the aircraftmen to attempt a break on their own, to feel they'd be handicapped by the wounded and barefoot sailors. On their return to the wrecked launch they had helped themselves to as much as they could carry in the way of food and clothing. They had blankets, spare shirts and a compass … corned beef, canned fish and tins of condensed milk. With the exception of defensive weapons, they could consider themselves well

equipped. Yet, despite all these hard-won advantages
of which, in fairness, Stanton now reminded them,
they were determined to make a joint escape.
Moreover, they insisted on dividing their stores with
the *Li Wo*'s empty-handed survivors. They entrusted
the responsibility of organising a rationing system
to Stanton, the senior officer. 'It's for all of us, sir.
Share and share alike!' Tait said.

Only the voice of the Malay, still pleading in pain
to be taken to hospital, disturbed the harmony.

'What do we do about him?' queried Maury.

'He'll stay here,' Stanton answered, reaching this
conclusion after considerable thought. It would be
impossible for the man to face the rigours of the
journey. The islanders were friendly, and of his
own race: best to leave him where he was. Nor
did the Malay object to the decision. He appeared
to welcome it. He cared for nothing, except his
mysterious pain. The very mention of walking sent
him into convulsions of agony.

They broke camp at 6.30 a.m. It was nearly
noon before they dared to halt. In the interval
they had trekked through a wilderness that would
have been difficult even for men in perfect physical
shape. They had waded chest-high through huge
fields of elephant grass. They had scrambled to the
top of a hill in an effort to spy out the land. They
had stumbled for miles along a razor-edged ridge.
And now, at its base, they were confronted by the
jungle. An unstirring sea.

At the start of the journey the *Li Wo* men had
wrapped their feet in sacking, but this had been a

poor substitute for shoes. Now as they lay in the shadow of a small wood, considering their next move, they nursed their bleeding feet, lacerated by countless stones and stumps. The pain reverberated again in Stanton's head. Neal had relapsed into delirium. They were utterly flaked out. Sick and sweating, they felt they could not move another step.

As an observation post, the hill had been a washout. Looking inland, their vision was blocked by jagged green-clad peaks and valley-mist, with no sign of huts or houses. Looking seawards, they were greeted by the sight of a Jap destroyer, patrolling slowly – and inquisitively – close to the spot where they had rested the previous night.

Their subsequent stumbling progress along the ridge had been made in single file, and unprotected from the blaze of the tropical sun. It had also been subject to constant interruption. Jap recce planes were persistently on the prowl and time after time their sudden appearance sent the tired men flopping on their bellies. They had not expected so much aerial activity: it seemed almost as though the Japanese were making a special search for them.

'Three and a half hours, that's all we've done,' reflected Stanton, reviewing the first lap with misgivings for the future. 'Three and a half hours, and weary enough for a lifetime.'

All the same, they were relieved to take the weight off their feet and enjoy a swig or two of the precious water ration. The wood gave the party cover from the air. It seemed too remote to be troubled by land patrols. Maybe, while they considered whether to brave the jungle or to skirt along its fringe until they discovered a more open route to the east, they could rest until dark. No virtue in rushing things.

Stanton was forced to reject the idea as soon as it was put forward. For an islander walked into their gathering.

He came upon them so suddenly that they were too startled to do anything more than stare. He passed them without a word – then switched his leisurely pace to a furtive haste that aroused immediately their old fears of betrayal.

'Shouldn't we follow him?' Tait asked.

'Fix him maybe,' Ginger Thompson suggested.

But Stanton shook his head. 'Then what? We can't murder him on suspicion. There's no hope for it. We'll just have to press on.'

Fear strengthened them. They did not stop until they had staggered off the ridge and trekked for miles into the vastness of the jungle.

In its darkness, its oppressive stillness, the jungle enveloped them with a security that at first bewildered them. It was so much greater than they'd ever expected. They seemed to have plunged into a world apart. But jungle-trekking proved to be hell's delight. With only a confusion of animal trails to break the otherwise impenetrable green curtain, it was impossible to find a direct route eastwards. Time after time they found themselves doubling back on their tracks, causing delays which might prove fatal. For although providing cover, the jungle was unfruitful. They could find nothing edible. Nothing, at least, that their untrained eyes could recognise as such. Every day they spent there would be a further drain on their rations.

Stanton decided reluctantly that the party must change its tactics: go westwards, back to the Strait. There they would have coconuts to supplement their diet, there would be possibilities, too, of salvaging food from the wreckage that Jap success had piled along the shores. On the other hand, the move would mean their having to face again the threat of the low-flying air patrols and of Jap troops watching the beaches.

'So you mean it's as you were?' Tough and resolute, LAC Gilbert always spoke his mind.

'Not quite,' said Stanton. 'This time, instead of lugging our gear around the island, we'll settle for a decent HQ near water and coconuts ... a sort of jumping-off point where we can take it in turns to spy out the land methodically, and replenish our food supplies before cracking eastwards again.'

He glanced at the ring of faces. At Gilbert's RAF colleagues – Tait, young Smead, the thoughtful Bagley, the steady Grant. At his own *Li Wo* comrades – Derbridge, Thompson and Maury. Did this note of confidence ring as falsely in their ears as it did in his own?

But, as before, he found himself supported by their loyalty and faith.

'I can't think of any better plan,' Gilbert said bluntly. 'So when do we go?'

The following day they came across a spectacle of horror worse than their most terrible nightmares. Their journey began when, from a high bluff, the RAF men spotted a wrecked launch. It was similar in class to their own. If there was any food left aboard her they reckoned they'd know where to find it.

It was not until they emerged cautiously from the concealing undergrowth, sweeping to the edge of the crescent beach surrounding the half-submerged launch, that they discovered that the beach was strewn with dead bodies ... hundreds of dead bodies ... corpses in various stages of decomposition.

And above them buzzed clouds of hungry flies.

For a moment the nerve of the fugitives broke completely. They recoiled towards the bushes as though hit by a gigantic invisible fist.

'Christ, let's get out of here!'

'We'll do no good by running,' Gilbert said roughly. His voice rallied them ... reminded them of their purpose.

His gruff manner reminded Stanton of Tom Wilkinson.

'Gilbert's right, lads,' he supported. 'Having come so far it's only sense to continue. Unless we want to share the fate of these poor devils.'

They walked along the sands, with their heads bent and their eyes to the ground, so that they should see no more than the immediate carnage at their feet.

But later, the extent of the horror numbed their humanity and they scanned the bodies for anything that might be useful to their own self-preservation. Afterwards, they felt guilty about this plundering and when fate turned sour on them, Derbridge saw it as a judgment.

Rain. Torrential rain. And the launch appeared to be as far away as ever. They still persevered, struggling against a drenching downpour driven furiously from a sky turned abruptly as black as night. But then they found themselves faced by yet another obstacle. The foaming mouth of a river, hidden until now by steep scrub. It forced them to strike into the bush, in the hope of crossing it at another point; but before they succeeded, and regained the beach again, they had waded waist-deep in swamp.

After seven hours of this terrible progress, Stanton decided they'd had enough. There was no refuge to go to, no roof beneath which they could shelter. There was only one thing for it ... they'd have to make their own.

Practical meaning was given to the idea by the recent discovery of a number of freshly cut poles. They erected these in the shape of an Indian tepee, bound together at the top by a service-belt. Then, over this improvised framework, they draped an abandoned fishing net, to which they secured several layers of thick palm leaves. To their surprise, the hut proved watertight, and stood up well against the wind.

Once in the dry, their first care was to get warm. The tropical heat had given place to the damp chill of an English November. They started a fire of twigs, and Stanton brewed coffee from cans acquired on the beach. Sweetened by condensed milk, it went down well. Later, one of the airmen produced some tobacco and a pipe. It was passed in turn to everyone in the circle, making the comparison to an Indian scene even closer. As they talked together in the snug twilight, and listened to the rain pattering futilely against their home, the men of the *Showboat* and their Air Force friends were at last almost contented.

Until they remembered the beaches ...

The beaches haunted them ... and they, though hatingly, were condemned to go back to them for loot. Daily their footsteps led them to fresh evidence of the magnitude of the tragedy. The tragedy that had overwhelmed the last refugee fleet. Of the eighty ships that had sailed before the *Li Wo*'s departure, over sixty had found their graves in these waters. Victims of the carnage were carried in on every tide. And now, gangs of Chinese came to rob and strip the dead.

Some of them were locals, but the majority were not. Japan had opened jail doors to celebrate the advent of the co-prosperity sphere: criminals, and unemployed labourers from all parts of the island were congregating on the Banka Strait. For Stanton's party their search for loot brought startling complications.

Obviously the journey to the beaches would become more dangerous each day, involve evasive detours, excruciatingly painful to their overtaxed bodies and torn feet. Yet the journey was absolutely necessary to their survival. With the exception of the coffee, the net results of their search had so far been meagre. The hundreds of tins and cases they recovered were so badly damaged that their contents were inedible. In such frustrating circumstances the thought of what might be waiting in the wrecked launch tormented them. Risk or no, they resolved that they must get at any provisions on board.

To avoid the Chinese they made a detour inland, into the fringes of the jungle. The going was terrible. There were ravines to cross, and thick scrub to fight their way through. Recent sores reopened on the heels of Stanton's feet. But Neal's were in even worse condition. Each step the New Zealander took was achieved laboriously. Encouraged by the rain, the flies increased and multiplied.

They had started their march in the early morning. It was not until 6 p.m. that they got to within striking distance of the launch, and Thompson, with two of the airmen, were free to begin the search.

Despite their tiredness they started with a will. The idea of reaching the launch had become almost obsessional to them. But there was less enthusiasm in the camp behind them. Worn out, two of the party were so much past caring that they began to talk of giving themselves up.

Rather than prolong their sufferings, they said they were ready to take the main road to Mundok, and take a chance on surrender.

Surrender? For the first time since the start of their adventure Stanton gave the pair the rough side

of his tongue. He knew they were not really 'anti'
– just temporarily down in the dumps. But, hell, he
exploded, so was everyone else. If it bloody well
came to it, he, Stanton, was down in the dumps. But
a serviceman didn't surrender except under hopeless
compulsion. 'And you,' he said, 'you aren't under
compulsion. You're scared by the ruddy rain!'

It was a cruel and unjust tirade directed at men
who had so far pulled their weight. But Stanton's
nerves were as frayed as theirs: he was furious in
case the surrender talk became infectious.

'Though if that's the way you feel,' he concluded,
'… that the journey's too tough for you … you can
damn well do as you like. Provided the Japs want
prisoners!'

By now the two men had changed their minds:
their complaints had been taken more literally
than they intended.

'Okay,' said Stanton, 'then let's call the subject
closed.'

Relationships in the camp were back to normal
by the time the launch-party returned.

They were carrying seventeen tins of corned
beef, plus such unexpected extras as a bucket,
a kettle, and a stewpot. Even more surprisingly
they produced a trio of chickens. Their pride of
achievement was intense and justified. The beef
and the kitchenware had been in the sunken part
of the launch, but undeterred they'd made an
underwater exploration to retrieve it.

'And the chickens?' queried Stanton. 'What
about the chickens?'

'The chickens,' said Thompson casually, 'we met with on the way here ...'

For starving men it was a banquet ... chicken, corned beef, and some onions found on the beach, cooked in the stewpot over a fire made from ship's timbers. And the strength given them by the food was put to good purpose. Their camping site was unsafe, and they had to find a spot more secluded: one that would serve as a more permanent base.

They started their trek in early morning. It was four in the afternoon when they blundered into what all of them regarded as the perfect hideout. It was sufficiently far from the beaches to be untroubled by the Chinese: or so they thought. Yet it was sufficiently near for them to forage for food. It consisted of two atlap shelters – native huts raised about three feet from the ground with bamboo poles for flooring. The shelters were well hidden, positioned at the foot of a vertical bank, which was higher than their roofs. On the other side they were well screened by the jungle. Only ten yards away was a running stream. A superb set-up. That night they celebrated their luck by opening another tin of coffee. The following morning they washed their clothes, bathed and attended to their leg and feet wounds. Not until three days later did they leave this snug hideout to look for coconuts along the beaches. But they found more than coconuts.

The coolie gang, as they later called a vicious group of new arrivals to the beach, came upon them when they were having lunch – a hunk of coconut each and a one-ninth share of a tin of condensed milk.

From a distance the Chinese made friendly gestures. But their manner changed when they came closer.

When Stanton asked them for information about the enemy, they replied by drawing their fingers significantly across their throats. The Japs, they said, would soon put paid to the British. Some of the survivors were wearing unbreakable wrist-watches. The coolies tried to pull them off. A bit of pushing and shoving followed before the Chinese eventually gave up.

Stanton's party were to see quite a lot of the coolie gang in the course of the next few days. And each time the attitude of these released criminals was more threatening than before. Their numbers, too, increased. On one expedition Thompson and Gilbert had to use clubs in order to drive them away.

At home, however, their life was steady, almost pleasant. On March 1st, Thompson even contrived to steal a pig. After the subsequent big meal, Stanton, comfortable in his billet, felt their luck was at last changing.

But the next day's events proved him wrong.

Stanton and Bagley left camp at 9 a.m. to restock the coconut larder. Just after noon they saw the coolie gang come on to the beach from the same direction as themselves. They hid in the bushes until the gang had passed and, after a little more effort, decided to head for home. They'd done quite well, collected a dozen nuts. Thoughts of pork had become uppermost in their minds.

Then they came across Grant's windcheater, lying at the entrance of the animal track that led towards their hideout.

'That's bloody peculiar,' Bagley said. 'Grant was staying in camp today.'

'Oh well,' Stanton said. 'I daresay it's simple enough. He probably decided to go on the food hunt too, and started after us.'

Bags said, uncertainly, 'Seems strange though – for him to dump his jacket like that. Shall I bring it in?'

'Good God, no. Best leave it where it is. Otherwise the poor chap will think someone's stolen it.'

They forgot about Grant's windcheater as they continued their tiring journey home. They forgot about Grant himself, until they met him.

He was lying on his back at the base of the ten foot bank screening the camp.

He was dead.

There was a bullet wound in the right side of his chest. Another bullet had lodged in his left groin.

Stanton felt his heart, merely as a formality. Death must have been instantaneous.

White faced, Bagley whispered, 'But where are the others?'

They shouted for them. But there was no reply.

CHAPTER TEN

Massacre In The Jungle

'Bloody silly,' Stanton told himself, as he moved towards the camp. 'For all you know they've murdered the whole damn bunch, and now they're waiting for you.'

Again he shouted, and this time thought he heard a reply. But it was incoherent and low-pitched.

Damn bloody silly. You could be walking into a trap. But his powers of reason seemed to have left him. He couldn't stop himself.

Then, as he came to the front of the shelters, he saw Neal Derbridge. He was doubled up like a jackknife, and clutching at his stomach.

'Neal, what the hell's happened?'

'That coolie gang, they ...' The New Zealander's voice became unintelligible.

'Steady, Neal.'

'They ... shot me in the guts.'

Stanton moved over to Tait. The airman had been wounded in both legs by the same bullet, which had passed through the right leg, then lodged in the left. Maury had been hit in the chest and was coughing blood.

Stanton and Bagley gazed around with horror. The camp was completely ransacked. Where had the others got to? Thompson, and Gilbert, and Smead?

A figure staggered out from the shadow of the forest. Young Smead.

'God, am I glad to see you,' the boy exclaimed with relief.

'And what have they done to you?'

'Got me in the thigh. But I managed to reach the trees. Next thing I heard was you calling. I suppose I must have passed out.'

'And Ginger? And Gilly? Do you know if they're O.K.?'

'I think there's a chance,' Smead answered. 'I saw them charge up the bank.'

Bit by bit they learned of the events which had led to this tragic scene.

The coolie gang they'd clashed with on the beaches had arrived at the camp an hour after Stanton and Bagley had left.

Swollen to twenty strong, and brandishing parangs and clubs, they had surrounded the Europeans, and proceeded to loot practically everything in sight.

Wrist watches, blankets, notecases and food ... they were grabbing the lot when Thompson and Gilbert reacted.

They laid furiously about them. But the odds were even more hopeless than they'd thought: for suddenly revolvers appeared, half a dozen of them.

And the Chinese started firing wildly at them.

At sound of the first shots, Thompson and Gilbert plunged for the bank. They climbed it barefoot, the bullets widely missing them. The Chinese turned their attention to the others, who'd stayed put.

One of the Chinese poked a revolver into Neal's stomach before pulling the trigger. The bullet entered below his navel, then turned and lodged itself in his thigh. Maury, too, was hit at point-blank range: impossible to miss. Tait was nursing his wounded legs when he felt a steel-cold sensation in his temple. A revolver barrel. His assailant was determined to make sure of him. But when the man fired there was only a loud click. He had exhausted his ammunition. 'Lucky for you,' Stanton said.

'Damn lucky,' the airman agreed. 'But I can't help wondering where they got their guns.'

'To hell with that,' said Stanton, busy bandaging. 'You mind your own business.'

'But maybe it is my business.'

Tait had recognised the revolvers as RAF issue. Was fretting in case 'they happened to be ours ... salvaged from the spot where we'd been fools enough to ditch them.'

Four seriously wounded men in a bandit-ridden wilderness ... four seriously wounded men whom the slightest mistake could kill ... Stanton and Bagley certainly had problems.

Stanton wrapped a thick wad of material around Neal's stomach to try and support it, bandaged Tait's leg up, bandaged Smead, and got his patients dressed. But the men needed more than elementary first aid. Grimly he made up his mind. They must try and deal with the Japs. He hated doing it. His years in the East had left him with little racial prejudice, but he had learned that all races did not observe the same ethical code.

It's quite probable, he thought, that the Japs won't be taking prisoners. And, even if they are, that they'll treat us damnably. A prisoner of war, in their eyes, is a lower form of life. A man who has fallen into the ultimate disgrace.

But whatever the Japs might do to them, one thing was certain now, that the wounded would die anyway if left to stay where they were.

'The only thing to do,' he said, 'is to get to Mundok as quickly as we can, and try to get you hospital treatment there.'

'But what about Maury?' Bags asked.

Stanton shifted uneasily, averting his eyes.

Problems ... problems ... but Maury was the saddest problem of all.

He was unable to stand, let alone walk. When they'd tried to hoist him to his feet he had almost choked to death, unable to breathe in an upright position. The bullet had probably penetrated a lung.

Yes ... what about Maury?

Had the seaman been on his own, Bags and he would have known what to do. They would have improvised a stretcher. Somehow they'd have contrived to take him with them, however difficult the going.

But there were the others to consider.

They couldn't carry a stretcher and help support the three others ... the walking wounded.

It was a physical impossibility.

But, God, how it hurt to leave him behind.

Not that – he argued – Maury would be left on his own for long. Ginger and Gilly were bound to return at nightfall to find out what had happened to their comrades.

All the same, he was deeply troubled by his decision.

He dreaded having to tell him.

'I expected it,' Maury said, with surprising calm. 'I don't see you've any choice.'

'You see,' said Stanton desperately, 'we'll leave you with plenty of water and bananas. And then Ginger and Gilly can pick you up, and follow on ...'

'Exactly. The rest will peg out if you don't get cracking now.'

The wounded man showed no resentment. He was almost tranquil.

Quietly Stanton said, 'Thank you.'

They said their goodbyes to Maury at four in the afternoon. The last they remembered of him was his feeble but brave attempt to wave.

Over the first lap the wounded behaved magnificently. Stanton was astonished at their uncomplaining trust. He was without a map, and the Chinese had stolen the compass. He was forced to rely on his memory for the whereabouts of a path which he'd once guessed might link up with the Mundok road. There was nothing definite about the route, any more than there was anything definite about what would happen if they ever reached the end of their journey. It was a matter of guesswork and hard going, with the hard going made even harder by heavy rain.

Yet, for all their struggle not to show it, the suffering of the wounded men soon became impossible to conceal. It was evident from the way Neal walked, surprisingly fast and way ahead of the column. At first young Bags, his escort, had been deceived by the pace; wondered whether the man was fitter than his wounds would suggest. But it was not reviving energy, but the agony of his wound that drove the New Zealander so far in front of the others. It hurt just as much to walk slowly as it did to walk fast; and he believed in a curious way that he was achieving something by walking fast. During the short resting periods he was unable to relax like the others. Unable to sit down owing to the nature of his wound, he had often to halt on his feet when its pain became too great. So he made up the time when he could.

For Tait, with both legs holed, and Smead, with a bullet in the thigh, it was not possible to do more than hobble, however hard they tried to hurry. Both leaned heavily on their sticks; and heavily on Stanton. But he – with his feet still desperately raw – did not envy young Bags his position in the front.

It was a miserable procession. As night fell and the moon rose, Stanton's thoughts were more troubled than ever before.

It was 10 p.m.

The path had merged into a wider track; everywhere overgrown, probably once a road, but for a long time disused. They were atrociously cold and their sodden clothes clung to them grotesquely.

For an hour they had been longing for sign of shelter: an atlap shed, a thick-leaved tree, almost anything would do. But there were no sheds, and the trees lay well back from the track. The forest would have provided cover for fit men, but its savagely meshed undergrowth made it impossible for the wounded to rest there. But they had to find somewhere to rest. And they had to rest now.

By midnight they were back on the path again, in the same straggling order as before.

At four in the morning their odd appearance and laborious progress was being watched by the entire population of an aroused kampong.

And they were still on the road, hours later, when, to their great surprise, a voice hailed them in English from the scrub.

By an extraordinary coincidence, they had come across a British LAC – a member of the same unit to which Bags and the others belonged.

The newcomer was called McCann. He had been on his own for three weeks. A determined character, still toughly cheerful, his hide-and-seek game across the island had taught him practically all there was to know about the attitude and behaviour of its Japanese masters. Mac's initial objective in refusing to surrender had been basic and simple. He wished to stay alive.

'The Nips answer to your raising your hands,' he graphically explained, 'is to slit open your guts.'

McCann had tried repeatedly to make an escape to Java. But the island boat owners were wary ... knew only too well what would happen to them should they allow their boats out. And now, of course, Java was no longer a refuge.

'I beg your pardon,' Stanton interrupted. 'You mean to tell us that Java has gone, too?' 'Christ, yes. Where have you been all this time?' Hong Kong ... Singapore ... Sumatra ... and now Java. Would the Jap triumphs never end?

The only thing sure to Stanton was that he could now ditch all regrets at sacrificing his escape chances to save the wounded. Escape chances didn't exist. There was no place to escape to ... nearer than Australia.

McCann said, 'So, I think, if you don't mind, that I'll join up with you lot.'

A mine of information, the new recruit informed them that Jap transport on the Mundok road was usually fairly heavy in the afternoon.

As a result of this, and his description of the savagery shown by individual groups to surrendering Europeans, Stanton decided that they could only use the road in the mornings.

He was anxious to stay well clear of the Japanese until the party succeeded in getting nearer to Mundok, or had managed to make contact with responsible authority.

'Our main hope ... maybe our only hope,' he said, 'is to get as close as possible to the enemy's top brass.'

It was a topsy turvy procedure, an escape plan in reverse. Instead of devoting their wits to the task of breaking out, they must plot and plan as to how best to get in. No wonder the wounded were bewildered.

They had thought, once the road was reached, they would merely have to wait: thumb, so to speak, the first Japanese truck that came. Yet now they were being urged to walk farther. In order to be taken prisoner they had to travel like hunted refugees. They didn't understand it.

It was only after they had got moving again that they appreciated the sense of Stanton's harsh decision.

In a ditch beside the road they found four corpses – bayoneted, mutilated, and now left to rot.

The corpses were in RAF uniform, their hands tied behind their backs.

They hid for the afternoon, but gained little comfort from their enforced rest. Asleep, they were terrorised by nightmares. Awake, each man was afraid for his life. McCann's forecast of heavy Jap traffic turned out to be depressingly accurate. Shortly after their discovery of the airmen's bodies, they had been nearly surprised by a fast truck filled with Jap infantry. They'd reached cover with only seconds to spare.

It was still raining. The mud in which they lay squelched dismally under the movement of their bodies. When they at last dragged themselves up, to face the rigours of the night march, it was difficult to distinguish the fit men from the wounded; their limbs were so stiff from weariness and exposure.

Their different degrees of suffering showed only when they began once more their stumbling trek.

After the first mile or so, Bagley became increasingly disturbed about Neal Derbridge. The New Zealander, he felt sure, was getting worse. He was talking deliriously as he walked along. At one moment he was aboard his first ship, the destroyer. At another he was clutching hold of the *Li Wo*'s upturned lifeboat. Sometimes he just howled in pain. But he marched on, a reeling automaton.

Stanton, meanwhile, was worried about Tait who, with bullet wounds in both legs, had been struggling along this roughest of trails for over twenty-four hours. How much longer could he keep going?

Stanton said aloud, 'Come on. You're doing fine. Every mile you make is a mile nearer safety ...'

It was at the end of their next rest period that Tait reached breaking-point.

'My legs,' exclaimed Tait, '... there's something wrong with my legs!'

'Sure,' soothed Stanton, coming to help him up, 'they've got a couple of bullet holes. Remember?'

'I mean my legs won't move,' Tait said. 'They've gone completely stiff.'

They had. As stiff as if encased in plaster. He couldn't bend them, no matter how hard he tried.

Stanton beckoned to McCann. 'Here, Mac, come and take a look at this.'

'My God,' exclaimed the airman. 'And now what do we do?'

Tait answered tersely, 'You must leave me – and press on,'

They couldn't do it. They wouldn't do it.

'But what about Maury?' Tait protested. 'We all of us left Maury.'

Maury. The memory still hurt, although they were sure that Ginger and Gilly would have found him by now.

'You know damn fine,' said Stanton, 'that we couldn't take Maury with us. But things are different now, with Mac here to give us a hand.'

They took turns in helping carry Tait's stretcher, improvised by them from branches and leaves.

But, despite their brave words, they found it a hell of a strain.

Stanton, Bagley and McCann were holding a conference together. Circumstances had forced them to change their plan again. They were meeting in a dilapidated native hut, as guests of its owner.

They had met him an hour earlier when the weight of the stretcher had become too much for them and they suddenly realised that they would fail in their attempt. They were too much encumbered to get nearer to Mundok unaided, without detection. The only hope was to get local help. But where to start?

It was just then that they met the Malay. The first living face they'd seen for hours. The coincidence of the timing and the fact that the man spoke English, had given them new hope. Almost before they realised what was happening they had found themselves explaining their position to him. And then he'd said confidently that he would find them transport, a covered cart that would get them undetected to Mundok.

But by now hours had passed since the Malay's departure ... hours of suspense, their fears and hopes alternating. The wounded had been laid at the back of the hut. Through a chink in the wall Stanton and Bagley kept uneasy watch on the road. But the only transport they saw belonged to the Japanese army.

All of the men, except Neal, were tormented by hunger. They'd eaten nothing for the past few days. Then Bagley discovered some rice ... rice that half-filled a filthy earthenware pitcher.

'It's stinking muck, real, genuine antique,' he said. All the same, he had a mouthful or two. So did Smead, Tait and McCann.

Stanton was more choosy. 'My God,' he exclaimed, 'it's bloody well crawling with maggots!'

Bagley said firmly, 'Better the maggots than nothing.'

Neal's delirium was by now almost continuous. Tait's legs were completely paralysed, though this gave him no relief from pain. Then, after nightfall, Bagley and Smead were sick: they threw up the maggot-ridden rice, and the sound of their vomiting echoed through the silent, cold darkness.

In a moment of coherence, Neal said: 'It's all up, Ronnie. I know that I'm going to die.'

The words came weakly, but with a dreadful air of certainty.

Stanton said, 'Don't be daft, Neal. We'll soon have you as right as rain.'

But the New Zealander shook his head. 'You bloody liar.'

Tears came into Stanton's eyes.

Neal said, echoing Tait. "There's no alternative. You chaps should leave us."

Stanton walked to the door of the hut, and stared out into the dawn. Grey clouds. Rain. The curving ribbon of the deserted road.

'I've made up my mind,' he said. 'We're not waiting for the Malay. I'll stop the first truck that comes. The very first truck. We'll just have to take our chance.'

He thought, 'And a hell of a chance that is.'

He remembered with horror the ditch and the bayoneted corpses. After bathing Neal and Tait, he groped into the rice pitcher.

He'd need some food in his guts to face what was to come.

Maggots and dust, the lot …

If the worst came to the worst, perhaps he'd be too sick to care.

Bagley, from the chink in the wall, exclaimed, 'A gang of coolies, and coming this way.'

Stanton took a look. They were a rough lot, like the murder gang of the beaches, and heading for the hut.

Earlier, the arrival of these looters would have caused alarm. Now no one cared. Stanton and Bagley allowed themselves to be searched: after all, they'd nothing to lose. They felt some anger at the way the gang handled the wounded: but the wounded were in such pain that they hardly noticed anyway. The Chinese search was thorough. They ransacked clothing and haversacks. They even broke into the water flasks in their hope of uncovering concealed treasure. At the end of it all they seemed quite astonished at the party's poverty. Although they did them no actual physical harm they laughingly made obscene gestures, indicating the likely fate of the survivors should the Japanese arrive.

'Seems that we can't do anything in comfort,' Bagley said, gloomily. 'Not even wait without these bastards sitting around and gloating.' He paused. 'Do you think it will be long, sir?'

It ... Stanton considered grimly the implications of the word. It ... the act of surrender ... the walk into the unknown.

'No, not very long,' he answered. 'It shouldn't be very long now.'

Yet when the moment, so tensely awaited, eventually arrived, he was taken by surprise. He was bathing Neal's head with a rag soaked in rainwater when the Chinese, excitedly gesticulating, ran from the hut. They, and not the survivors, had been the first to hear the distant hum of the truck. Now they were getting out of the line of fire ... taking up positions beside the road.

He was walking to his death, he was almost sure of it. His brain was numb, his legs were taut with fear. The truck had pulled up at the end of the road, and the coolie Chinese, laughing and excited, were pointing to the hut. He bowed his head ...

He began mechanically to count his paces and was aware that the Japanese had turned from the coolies and were looking at him. He didn't see them do this. He only felt their stare. He kept his eyes down, focused on the muddy ditch in front of him, unable to look up.

The lush green undergrowth opposite the verandah swam in the noon haze, and he thought with astonishment, 'How extraordinary, after all we've been through together ... to die so very far from the sea.'

Birds rose, alarmed, around him, and insects buzzed over the harsh, unyielding grass. His head was aching, his naked feet were gashed with thorns, the maggoty rice brought violent stomach pains.

Three weeks since the *Li Wo*, the ship they called the *Showboat*, had sailed on her last incredible voyage. Nineteen days since she'd fought the Jap armada single-handed. Nineteen days, and each of them a lifetime.

The Japs were shouting at him, and yet he could hardly hear them: his thoughts were of the past. He could almost smell the fumes of Neal's four-inch gun (made in Japan) ... could almost hear the crash of the timbers as the little steamer rammed her bows into the transport's belly.

Some day, he thought, they'll tell the *Li Wo*'s story. Some day they'll talk about her and praise her fight. But her fame lay in the future, and he probably wouldn't live to see it.

He came out into the road, and put up his hands.

CHAPTER ELEVEN

Banzai

The jolting of the truck and the rough handling by the Japanese proved too much for Neal Derbridge. He died in Stanton's arms as the prison gate creaked open. Tait died three weeks later. Decent diet and decent treatment could have saved him. And Maury? Maury, though none of them knew it, had probably died first. Ginger Thompson and Gilly had been captured by a Japanese patrol the day after the coolies' attack on the camp. So Maury had died on his own. Of the *Li Wo*'s original complement, only nine men remained alive. And only two of these came from Stanton's party of four. The remainder were the men he and Manston had left behind in the shattered lifeboat. Under the leadership of Petty Officer Lofty Rogers, they had managed to keep her afloat, until they were picked up by a naval whaler with oars and a sail.

It was with these comrades that Stanton, through four years of horror, wrote down the facts of the *Li Wo*'s last fight and the adventures of her survivors and their RAF comrades.

They were facts written down on scraps of

exercise book paper taken from a gutted Javanese schoolhouse ... scraps sometimes concealed in Stanton's only prison clothes, a loincloth ... sometimes blatantly displayed as *benjo*, the Japanese word for lavatory paper. They were facts which earned for the *Li Wo*, the humble *Showboat*, thirteen awards and commendations, and the title of 'the most decorated small ship in the Navy'.

Banzai? No. Never, you bastards. This was the faith of the *Li Wo*'s survivors when they set about their self-appointed, dedicated task.

It was like an echo of gruff Tom Wilkinson, posthumous VC.

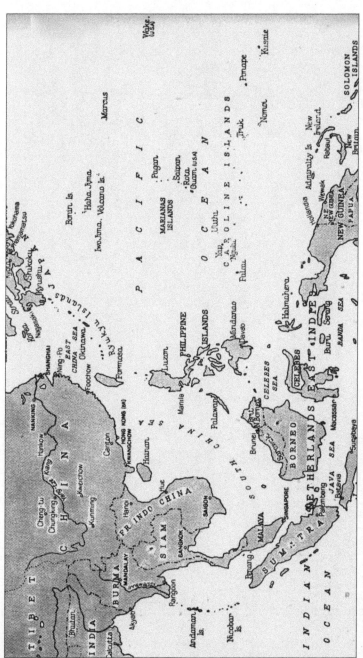

The Pacific theatre, showing the islands of Iwo Jima and Okinawa.

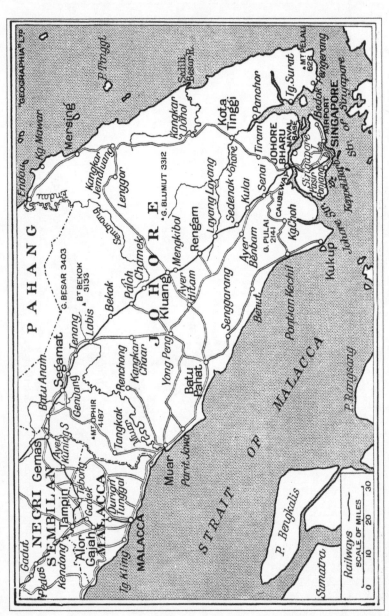

Southern Malaya and Singapore. Map of the country over which British troops fought to stem the advance of the Japanese.

List of Abbreviations

AA – Anti-Aircraft
AB – Able Seaman
A/S – Anti-Submarine
CO – Commanding Officer
CPO – Chief Petty Officer
GHQ – General Headquarters
HQ – Headquarters
LAC – Leading Aircraftsman
Lt – Lieutenant
MTB – Motor Torpedo Boat
NCO – Non-Commissioned Officer
QM – Quartermaster
RAF – Royal Air Force
RNR – Royal Navy Reserve
RNVR – Royal Navy Voluntary Reserve
SBA – Sickbay Attendant
W/T – Wireless Telegraphy
VC – Victoria Cross